ONE MINUTE MOTIVATION
for Mindset

Change Negative Thinking, Overcome Self-Doubt, and Create a Life You Love Daily

LYNN LOK-PAYNE

WELLMINDED
MEDIA

Library of Congress Control Number: 2025921251

ISBN: 9798993334103 (hardback), 9798990245891 (paperback), 9798993334110 (ebook)

Published by WellMinded Media
3941 Park Drive, Ste 20-559, El Dorado Hills, CA 95762

www.LynnLokPayne.com
Designed by McKenna Payne
Printed in The United States of America
First Edition: 2026
1 2 3 4 5 6 7 8 9 10

For seekers everywhere
who know that change begins within—
your mindset and the story you tell yourself
shape the life you live.

Contents

What is Mindset?

Mindset shapes everything—how we go about our daily lives, connect with others, grow through different seasons, and the way in which we view ourselves and the world. Our lives are a mirror for what we focus on and believe in.

When we give our attention to possibilities and ground our thoughts in the present moment, we make room for peace. In this space, there's no mental chaos or overthinking. Here we find clarity, calm, and awareness.

But it's so easy to get distracted and drift away from this state. Our minds race. Our thoughts loop. Our emotions spiral. Doubt, worry, and fear creep in. This isn't weakness or personal flaw; it's biology. Our brains are wired to scan for threats, which is a survival mechanism from ancient times that still exists today. However, the very things that once kept us safe now often hold us back.

So much of our thinking isn't even based on truth. It's formed through fear, assumptions, false narratives, and outdated stories we've repeated for years. The good news is that with awareness, we can shift our thinking and create a more empowering mindset.

This book is a guide to help you do just that.

It's not about striving for perfection or never thinking a negative thought again. That's not realistic. It's just about becoming more aware of your inner dialogue, challenging what no longer serves you, and gently replacing it with something kinder, truer, and more supportive.

You can't change what you're not aware of. But once you pay attention and notice your mindset, you can begin recognizing what keeps you small and start investing in what is worthy of your joy. By observing your thoughts instead of believing in every one, fear loosens its grip and stress soften. That's when clarity returns.

As you read through these pages, you'll learn how to pause, reframe, and redirect your mindset to encourage growth, rather than limit it. You'll make small shifts from doubt to happiness, fear to confidence, and blockages to possibilities.

With this, you'll build genuine self-trust, take action toward your desires, and open up to a more peaceful, powerful way of being.

Let's begin.

Remember this: Question your thoughts,
doubt your assumptions, and challenge your beliefs
because not everything you think is true.

CHAPTER 1

Happiness

You Are the Priority, Not the Afterthought

True happiness lives inside us.
It's not something we find outside of ourselves.

I cultivate
my own happiness.

Happiness might come to us unexpectedly, but it's typically a habit we can nurture and grow. The more we implement it, just like anything else, the more likely it'll become routine. It all starts with choosing what to focus on.

Happiness expert, Dr. Bruce Hood, explains what he calls "happiness hacks."[1] These hacks are taught in the Science of Happiness coursework at the University of Bristol and can be applied to daily life. They include:

- Performing acts of kindness.
- Savoring one's experiences.
- Practicing feeling grateful.
- Being physically active.
- Exploring mindfulness and other meditation techniques.
- Increasing social connections and initiating conversations with people you don't know.
- Deliberately drawing attention to the events and aspects of your day.

I also find that self-reflection, delving into inspiration, and savoring the present moment brings joy.

Happiness is up to you; you get to decide if you want to be happy. And this knowledge is irreversible. Once you know that you can create your own happiness, there's no going back. You have the power.

Takeaway: Happiness is a decision, a choice, and a habit we create.

> "Very little is needed to make a happy life;
> it's all within yourself, in your way of thinking."
> **— MARCUS AURELIUS**

A positive mindset is a good way to jumpstart my day.

Do you focus on the positive or the negative? Do you wake up in the morning thinking, *Today will be great*, or, *I've just got to get through the day*? Feel the difference? Your thoughts shape the course of your day.

If I begin my day focusing on what's working or what I'm grateful for, my attitude improves. However, if I start with a negative mindset and place my attention on everything that's wrong, it can snowball and monopolize the rest of my day. Positivity boosts productivity.

I build a foundation for success by starting my mornings with expecting a good day. I find it helpful to repeat positive affirmations. To start your day off right, consider these statements:

- I can adopt a more positive outlook, mindset, and perspective.
- I will seize the day and make the most of every opportunity.
- I know I can handle today's challenges, no matter how loud the chaos gets.
- I am confident and trust in my abilities.

Each day brings in fresh opportunities if we are open to receiving them. Even if things don't go as planned, we're better equipped to roll with the punches when we have a positive mindset.

Takeaway: Begin each day looking for the good.

> "When you wake up every day, you have two choices.
> You can either be positive or negative; an optimist
> or a pessimist. I choose to be an optimist.
> It's all a matter of perspective."
> — **HARVEY MACKAY**

By starting the day with self-care, I design a life that is more balanced.

Begin with self-care for a better day. Most mornings, I read personal development books and go for a walk. This boosts my happiness and makes me feel empowered.

By launching into the day engaging in positive activities, such as meditation, reading, exercising, or gratitude journaling, I prioritize my well-being.

Do what replenishes and matters most to you. This will help you to feel more balanced and in-charge throughout the rest of your day.

Takeaway: Take time each day to connect with your well-being.

"Self-care is the fuel for everything you do."
— MCKENNA PAYNE

I boost my happiness by engaging in healthy activities.

We can increase happiness by stimulating dopamine, a key player of the brain's reward system. Known for its feel-good effect, dopamine plays a role in habits and reinforcement.

According to the Cleveland Clinic, "Our brains are hard-wired to seek out behaviors that release dopamine in our reward system. When you're doing something pleasurable, your brain releases a large amount of dopamine. You feel good and you seek more of that feeling."[2]

You can naturally boost dopamine by engaging in soul-nourishing activities like yoga, laughter, or meaningful conversations. These joyful moments make you feel good, creating the building blocks for a healthier, happier you.

Every step you take creates momentum. By making purposeful choices, you're not only making progress, but you're also training your brain to experience more joy.

Takeaway: Take positive actions to improve your mood.

"Start where you are. Use what you have.
Do what you can."

— ARTHUR ASHE

When I add variety to my day, I discover more about myself.

How long has it been since you changed your daily routine? Maybe it's time to try something new to raise your happiness levels. "Our results suggest that people feel happier when they have more variety in their daily routines," explains Catherine Hartley, an assistant professor in New York University's Department of Psychology.[3]

"The results showed that on days when people had more variability in their physical location—visiting more locations in a day and spending proportionately equitable time across these locations—they reported feeling more positive: 'happy,' 'excited,' 'strong,' 'relaxed,' and/or 'attentive.'"[4]

Get out and explore by switching up your routine. Go to a different farmer's market, grocery store, or lunch spot. Take an art class, read in various genres, or visit a new locale. You may just find something you love to do.

Takeaway: Create variety in your routine.

> "Variety is the spice of life."
> — WILLIAM COWPER

I make happiness a priority by doing things that bring me joy.

Happiness is a product of our mindsets, intentions, and beliefs. It's not what happens to us. It's how we perceive it.

We can create reminders for the things that fulfill us by making a Happy List. Basically, you write down situations, events, people, or places that bring you joy. Next to each item, describe how engaging in the activity makes you feel, whether it's joyful, peaceful, excited, loving, etc.

Incorporate Happy List items into your daily or weekly activities, like enjoying a cup of tea, talking to an uplifting person, or looking at a picture of your favorite place. Refer to these items if you need to boost your bliss. Alternatively, visualize them and embrace the enjoyable feelings.

The benefits not only help during the practice, but also throughout the rest of your day. It's important to focus on and prioritize the parts of life that bring you joy.

Takeaway: Incorporate things you enjoy into your life.

"The more you praise and celebrate your life, the more there is in life to celebrate."

— OPRAH WINFREY

Music instantly boosts my mood and energy.

Music has the power boost your mood, especially cheerful tunes. I know if I'm feeling in a funk, listening to a fun song helps to pull me out of the blues. And there's research behind it.

Music activates the reward center in the brain and releases dopamine.[5] This can improve your mood and overall well-being. Music helps you relax, slows your breathing, and calms the nervous system.[6]

"Research has shown that listening to music can reduce anxiety, blood pressure, and pain as well as improve sleep quality, mood, mental alertness, and memory," states John Hopkins Medicine.[7]

So, turn up the volume and listen to your favorite tunes, sing, or play an instrument. You can also create a happy playlist to bump up your mood. It's a wonderful tool to use if you are feeling down. At the end of this book, you'll find a happy playlist which contains catchy songs to get your day going.

I can't imagine a world without music. Song lyrics share stories, building bridges between people and giving voice to emotions. My life is happier, brighter, and more meaningful because of music. Naturally, I included the following quote by my favorite artist, Sir Elton John.

Takeaway: Music is my happy place.

> "Music has healing power."
>
> — ELTON JOHN

Laughter fills my soul with great happiness.

A burst of laughter can quickly brighten your mood. Laughter not only makes you feel better, but also truly is good medicine. "Laughter strengthens your immune system, boosts mood, diminishes pain, and protects you from the damaging effects of stress. Nothing works faster or more dependably to bring your mind and body back into balance than a good laugh," states mental health nonprofit, HelpGuide.org.[8] Seek out positive and humorous content. Sharing laughter multiplies its joy and benefits everyone involved.

Say cheese! Smiling is the beginning of laughter. Nicholas Coles, a Stanford research scientist, led a study and found, "Strong evidence that posed smiles can, in fact, make us happier."[9] The researchers discovered "a noticeable increase in happiness from participants mimicking smiling photographs or pulling their mouth toward their ears."[10]

Takeaway: Smile more, laugh loud, laugh often.

> "Nothing in the world is as contagious as laughter and good humor."
>
> — CHARLES DICKENS

Recalling happy memories is a tool I use to bring me joy.

Remembering happy times makes you happier.

According to author Gina Vild on Psychology Today, "The health benefits of revisiting positive memories extend far beyond temporary jolts of happiness. Studies have shown that intentionally recalling happy experiences can help to disrupt negative thinking patterns, alleviate anxiety, and even lower cortisol levels."[11]

Here are a few of her suggestions for creating habits to reminisce over good times:[12]

- Instead of counting sheep, count happy memories. This induces relaxation and joy.
- Share "remember when" stories with loved ones to strengthen bonds and relive the laughter.
- Capture joyful moments on paper to keep them alive.
- Revisit old photos to recall treasured times that bring smiles.
- Send a heartfelt note to someone who brightens your life. It'll uplift both of you.
- Use sensory prompts like music, scents, or flavors to unlock warm memories. For instance, the smell of cookies can transport you right back to feelings of home and comfort.

Takeaway: Remembering happier moments boosts our current happiness levels.

"The next best thing to the enjoyment
of a good time is the recollection of it."
— JAMES LENDALL BASFORD

I create more joy by focusing on the building blocks of happiness.

Happiness consists of three major components. These include enjoyment, satisfaction, and purpose, according to Arthur C. Brooks, a Harvard professor and social scientist.[13]

Here's a summary each part:
- Enjoyment: It may look like pleasure, or feeling good, though this is not fully correct. It takes a nod from pleasure, but adds communion and consciousness. Brooks gives a great example of a Thanksgiving feast. While the food itself is pleasurable, the true enjoyment comes from creating memories and sharing meals.
- Satisfaction: It's the excitement of achieving something you've worked for, but it needs to include a little suffering to be satisfying. Yet, satisfaction, as with enjoyment, is short-lived.
- Purpose: We can survive without the previous two for a period, but without purpose, life's difficulties become harder and we feel lost. Purpose gives our lives' meaning, leading to hope and inner peace. The aim shouldn't be to remove suffering, but to use it for personal growth.

My suffering led me to writing. I transformed my trauma into a message of resilience. I find this work incredibly rewarding, both personally and when people tell me how it's impacted their lives. It's become my purpose.

Takeaway: Happiness can be found when we succeed in overcoming.

> "Life is never made unbearable by circumstances, only by lack of meaning and purpose."
> — VIKTOR FRANKL

Finding my purpose
is a journey of self-discovery.

Purpose is about discovering what is important to you. It doesn't need to revolutionize the world; it's simply a reason to start each day.

Even small, meaningful pursuits, like gardening, can be very fulfilling. Of course, gardening does help our environment, so a small-scale purpose can also lead to a larger impact, too.

There have been times in my life where I've asked myself, *What's my purpose?* and *Why am I here?* These questions come up when I'm facing challenges, after upsetting experiences, or at a crossroads—when I'm struggling to see where to turn and what to do next.

That's when I have to take a step back and examine my life. *Am I doing things that align with my core values and passions?* If the answer is no, I re-evaluate my decisions and their impact on my happiness.

Purpose can change over time. Regularly check in with yourself to see if anything has changed. Take time to reflect, journal, and explore new interests if you are feeling unfulfilled or something just feels off. Decisions become easier when you're clear on who you are and what you want, either supporting your purpose or not.

Takeaway: When we examine ourselves, we discover our purpose.

"Knowing yourself is the beginning of all wisdom."

— ARISTOTLE

I'm choosing to be happy in all that I do.

Happiness is a natural result of using our talents and passions. However, sometimes we must do things we dislike, such as cleaning. In these moments, we can still find a little joy by changing our mindset. Rather than, *I don't want to clean*, try, *A clean house uplifts me.*

A simple shift in language can make a big difference. Phrases like *I have to, I need to,* or *I must* can signal obligation rather than desire. They often point to hidden feelings of burden, pressure, or even resentment. Over time, this can leave you feeling drained, disconnected, or like something vital is missing.

On the contrary, phrases such as *I want to, I get to,* or *I'm inspired to* communicate a sense of excitement, curiosity, and freedom. These feelings can energize you to succeed.

Additionally, we can cultivate more enjoyment by not only focusing on the end goal, but also discovering ways in which we can make the process better. For example, we can make cleaning more fun by listening to music or audiobooks.

We spend most of our time in the journey, rather than at the finish line, so we might as well enjoy it. If we can find peace in the doing, then we can live a happier, more fulfilling life. As Albert Schweitzer said, "Success is not the key to happiness. Happiness is the key to success. If you love what you are doing, you will be successful."

Embark on the pursuit of your happiness, a path paved with self-discovery, enthusiasm, and joy.

Takeaway: You make your own happiness.

"The Constitution only guarantees you the right to pursue happiness. You have to catch it yourself."

— BENJAMIN FRANKLIN

When I'm optimistic,
I naturally increase my happiness.

Happiness is fleeting. However, if we can look on the bright side of life's circumstances, we can create better outcomes. Even when we can't change something, a positive perspective helps us not to be torn down by it.

It's always our perspective of a situation, not the situation itself, that determines our state of being. If we want to develop more happiness, we must change our outlook.

Look for the good or the lesson, no matter how small, in everything. Happiness is not something we go out and find. It's created in our own mind. As the Dalai Lama said, "Choose to be optimistic. It feels better."

So, the next time you're feeling down, try to find something to be thankful for. It's the quickest way I've found to feel better.

Takeaway: Happiness is not external. It's created by you.

"My optimism has helped me through some hard times. If you try to send out good things, good things come back to you."

— JAN BRETT

My optimism improves my well-being.

Optimism has many advantages. "Studies show that optimists adopt healthier habits. They have a lower stress level and a more stable cardiovascular system than average, and you have a stronger immune system. You're happier, have fewer health complaints, healthier relationships and live an average of seven and a half years longer than average."[14] Wow, that's a lot of good reasons to look at the glass as half-full.

Takeaway: Focus on the good. It's better for your health.

"A pessimist sees the difficulty in every opportunity; an optimist sees the opportunity in every difficulty."

— WINSTON CHURCHILL

I create my own joy.

Joy is not found externally; it originates from within. True joy comes from being at peace with who you are right now. Not when you get the new job, find the relationship, or lose the weight.

Once you feel this, there is no longing to fill this need with anything outside of yourself. You have enough. And most importantly, YOU are already enough.

Yes, you can be happy about taking a trip or getting a new car, but these emotions are fleeting. Perhaps a year from now, the novelty of a new car will fade and a car will just be a car. However, once you find your inner joy, you know that material possessions won't bring long-lasting bliss.

Inner joy is about knowing in this spot, at this moment, is where you find happiness because it lives inside you. Dig in, nourish, and grow these roots. You are ready to bloom.

Takeaway: The root of joy lies within oneself.

"You are the one that possesses the keys to your being. You carry the passport to your own happiness."

— DIANE VON FURSTENBERG

Fear

Break Through Mental Blocks and Conquer Self-Doubt

When you rise above the fears
and doubts of your inner voice,
you let your own greatness emerge.

I conquer my fear through taking action.

What is fear? Merriam-Webster describes fear as, "An unpleasant often strong emotion caused by anticipation or awareness of danger."[15]

Fear is a universal experience and natural response. It protects us from potential dangers, for instance, walking too close to the edge of a mountain. We can also experience fear when something matters deeply, like an actor's pre-performance anxiety. Yet, the majority of our fears are just worries of possible outcomes and not the reality of the situation. This may impede progress.

Fear is a mental block that stands between you and what you desire. One way to reduce fear is by taking action. I know this can be difficult, but once you confront your fears, you may realize they weren't as daunting as you imagined.

Let me give you a personal example. My family and friends wanted to go ziplining and I stayed back because I was afraid. However, seeing how much they loved it, I wished I hadn't let my fear take over. So, the next time the opportunity came up, I went, despite my fear. As I climbed the first platform, my heart raced. The thought of being attached to a clip so high up, dangling in the air, scared me. But I took a leap of faith and pushed through my fear.

And you know what? I ended up loving it. This experience showed me something important: I had not only created the worry, but I also had the power to shift it. I realized it wasn't the action itself that was holding me back, but the false what-ifs swirling around it.

Now, when I feel hesitation rise, I ask, *What's really behind this feeling?* and *What's the possibility that it'll happen?* These simple questions help me move through the fear instead of being frozen by it.

Takeaway: Action eases fear.

> "Life opens up opportunities to you,
> and you either take them
> or you stay afraid of taking them."
>
> — JIM CARREY

I intentionally envision positive outcomes.

Our brains have a natural tendency to focus on the negative. This negativity bias, which originated from ancient times, was a survival mechanism to protect ourselves from potential threats, like tigers chasing us.[16] (Yes, that would be frightening!) We needed to be alert to spot any warning signs.

Today, many of these thinking threats are just incorrect narratives running wild. The more we ruminate on them, the more we may spiral. We tend to make these stories seem far worse than they actually are. With a bit of focus, we can navigate away from the worst-case scenario toward a more favorable outcome.

By reframing negative thoughts, we can build stronger self-narratives and achieve better results.

Takeaway: Create more empowering stories.

"Life can show up no other way
than the way in which you perceive it."
— NEALE DONALD WALSCH

Understanding and addressing my fear helps me to release it.

We are born with only two innate fears: the fear of falling and the fear of loud sounds.[17] Therefore, most fears are learned behaviors that become beliefs.

Many of our beliefs are shaped in childhood, often influenced by a parent, relative, or another adult in our lives. "Once formed, these beliefs are stored, rarely questioned and all but forgotten—yet they provide the compass we live by as adults. Every time something in our life matches the subconscious belief we hold, that belief is further confirmed."[18]

If a parent had a fear of failure, we might also develop this worry. Or if we constantly heard the narrative that money is hard to come by, we may develop a scarcity mindset and become fearful of money.

Once we understand that fear is largely a learned behavior, we can undo its influence by first asking, *Are these claims accurate?* If not, then we revise our beliefs by telling a different story with phrases similar to *I can do this* or *I have the power to create new opportunities.* This reframes our scarcity mindset to an abundant one.

Takeaway: I have the ability to revise my fears and create new beliefs.

> "Nothing in life is to be feared.
> It is only to be understood."
>
> — MARIE CURIE

I won't let the fear
of rejection stop me.

Rejection is a common fear. We have an internal desire to be accepted and included. This is part of our basic human need to connect with and belong to a group.[19] When we feel rejected or excluded, whether real or imagined, it casts a long shadow, affecting our relationships, careers, and ability to achieve goals.

Prior rejection, especially in our developmental years when we are forming our core beliefs, can deeply affect our confidence and self-esteem, causing us to avoid close relationships to protect ourselves from further hurt. We also could display needy behaviors and become people-pleasers, thus valuing external approval over authentic, personal worth.

Fear of rejection often stops us from trying, which validates the fear, proving us right. So, what are our options? "Working with our fear of rejection or actual rejection involves opening to our felt experience. If we can have a more friendly, accepting relationship with the feelings that arise within us as a result of being rejected, then we can heal more readily and move on with our lives."[20]

By exploring where our doubts come from, we can challenge outdated beliefs and replace harsh self-talk with kinder, more supportive language that's rooted in compassion. "As we become less afraid of what we're experiencing inside—that is, less afraid of ourselves—we become less intimidated by rejection and more empowered to love and be loved."[21]

Takeaway: Find out the why behind the fear.

"I take rejection as someone blowing a bugle in my ear to wake me up and get going, rather than retreat."

— SYLVESTER STALLONE

My dreams are worth the risk of disappointment.

The fear of being disappointed stops us from taking chances, which can become a self-fulfilling prophecy.

We can trace some fears back to past events that we're anxious to not repeat. For example, if we fell off while learning how to ride a bike, we may think it'll happen again, so we don't try. It's all tied to emotions, so the stronger the emotion, the more intense the fear of being let down. Just because it happened in the past, does not mean it will again. Pick up the bike and take another ride.

By giving into fear, we'll simply invite more of it into our lives. Don't let the past defeat you or dictate the future. Your dreams lie on the other side of your fears.

Takeaway: Beyond my fear, my dreams await.

"The only place where your dream becomes impossible is in your own thinking."
— ROBERT H. SCHULLER

I will not let
my past define me.

Often, we become consumed by the narrative of our own life experiences. The weight of being wronged, mistreated, cheated on, ignored, neglected, overlooked, wounded, and even forgotten hangs heavy on our hearts. When we keep retelling these stories to ourselves, it feels as though the past is happening all over again right now. It's the same as dragging around a huge suitcase all the time—the extra baggage will make current experiences feel needlessly tiring and overwhelming.

Release the old burdens and shape a more empowering storyline. By updating the narrative, you will create a different future. As Louise Hay stated, "It's only a thought and a thought can be changed." Your past only defines you if you allow it to. You are the author of your own life's story. If you desire a different outcome, write a new narrative. You hold the pen.

Takeaway: Leave past wounds and write a new chapter.

"Fear prevents us from moving outside the comfort—
or even the familiar discomfort—of what we know.
It's nearly impossible to achieve our highest vision
for our lives as long as we are being guided by our fears."
— DEBBIE FORD

My experiences give me an advantage, proving I have the power to defeat my fears.

When recalling fears that you've overcome, let them fuel your determination to conquer current worries. The obstacles you've worked through have been instrumental in your achievements and progress.

Imagine you have a phobia of hiking up a mountain. You could start by taking short hikes up hills to lessen your fear. Then, once you succeed in that, you'll have an advantage the next time something similar happens because you know that you are capable. Past wins build future courage to confront your fears.

Takeaway: Facing fear builds future resilience.

"The road to overcoming your fears
could lead you to unbearable places
but sometimes such gives you an edge
than nothing else could give."

— OSCAR AULIQ-ICE

I'm challenging my fear by venturing beyond my comfort zone.

When we attempt to try something new, fear can surface because walking into unfamiliar territory triggers stress and anxiety. Only when we confront our comfort zones do we truly grow.

At first, we might be fearful of what may happen. Once we get to the middle, when we are in the thick of it and still learning, we'll experience challenges and learning curves. However, the end could bring unexpected rewards. There's a certain satisfaction that comes from taking the leap. This fosters faith, both now and in future endeavors. And the more we explore, the easier it becomes.

Move beyond the comfort zone, stretch your capabilities, and push boundaries. Perseverance not only helps you achieve your goal, but it also changes you. You are not the same person who began the journey. You've made incredible progress.

Takeaway: Trying new things may lead to some of our greatest life moments.

"The fears we don't face become our limits."

— ROBIN SHARMA

I am brave enough to face my fears.

Merriam-Webster's dictionary definition of bravery is, "The quality or state of having or showing mental or moral strength to face danger, fear, or difficulty."[22] So bravery is not the absence of fear, it's facing it.

We're only limited by our fearful thinking and how we interpret situations. Take a look at fear and challenge it. Ask questions like, *Why am I afraid?* or *Where is this fear coming from?* Many times, the answers are not based on facts, but are just stories of potential realities we've created in our minds.

One piece of advice for overcoming fear is to start small. Don't get overwhelmed by the whole picture. Instead, break it down. Every step doesn't need to be known in advance. All that's needed right now is to make the next step. Yes, I know it's scary. Tune into your inner wisdom, not your fear, and it will lead you. It knows the way.

Takeaway: Focus on one piece at a time.

"And one has to understand that braveness
is not the absence of fear but rather the strength
to keep on going forward despite the fear."
— PAULO COELHO

I grow braver
with every step.

Familiarity helps to decrease fear. This is the basis of exposure therapy, which is built on the idea of exposing someone to the fear slowly in a safe environment.

For example, if you are afraid of spiders, a therapist might start with a fake spider. Then, after some time, work up to exposing you to a real spider. And eventually, may even have you touch a spider.

According to Stanford neuroscientist, Philippe Goldin, "Exposure is hands down the most successful way to deal with phobias, anxiety disorders, and everyday fears of any sort."[23] The article continues to state, "Study after study has revealed that, whether it's sky-diving or public speaking, simply repeatedly exposing ourselves to the thing we're afraid of—ideally in a positive way—gradually brings down the physiologic fear response until it's gone, or at least manageable."[24]

Identify a situation that causes you slight discomfort or fear, like voicing your ideas at a meeting. Start by offering one brief comment. Once the meeting is over, congratulate yourself for having the courage to speak up. At the next meeting, aim to provide a little more input.

Keep working at it, and as your confidence grows, you'll find it easier to contribute. The fear may still persist, however, it no longer controls you.

Takeaway: Take baby steps and slowly expose yourself to what holds you back.

"If we are afraid of things in our lives and they are not dangerous and could even be good for us, then exposing ourselves to them is the way forward."
— MICHAEL A. SOUTHAM-GEROW

I become more confident when I share my ideas, opinions, and solutions.

Many times, we don't speak up because we're afraid of what people will think. Self-doubt creeps in as we worry that we lack expertise or fear that others will dismiss our ideas as foolish. We've all been there. We need to remember that our opinions are valuable and should be considered. Who knows? We may just have the best idea.

Speaking up builds confidence and improves communication skills. Yes, there will be times when miscommunication happens or we fail to get our message across. Everyone experiences these moments. That's okay. It'll strengthen our skills for the next time.

Don't be afraid to speak up. You are important and your message is meant to be heard.

Takeaway: Speak up!

"Speak your mind, even if your voice shakes."
— MAGGIE KUHN

My confidence in public speaking increases with practice.

Many people are anxious when it comes to speaking publicly, so they avoid eye contact, yet this increases the anxiety.[25] Why are we nervous when observed? It dates back to prehistoric times when being watched might signal a predator's presence.[26] If all eyes are on us, we can feel that we're being criticized, judged, or are in danger.

"Our brains have transferred that ancient fear of being watched onto public speaking. In other words, public-speaking anxiety is in our DNA. We experience public speaking as an attack. We physiologically register an audience as a threatening predator and mount a comparable response," states Sarah Gershman, executive speech coach and professor at Georgetown University.[27]

Gershman discusses three steps for public speaking:[28]
1. Think about the audience first before you prepare your topic. By identifying the audience—who are they, why they're here, and what they need—you'll be speaking on common ground.
2. Refocus the brain right before you speak. Tell yourself, *Brain, this presentation is not about me. It is about helping my audience.* It takes about four to six presentations for the brain to begin to believe it.

3. Make eye contact with one individual, not the whole crowd. Focus on one person per thought. Using this technique three consecutive times lowers anxiety.

Bonus tip: Try to connect with the people on the sides of the room. Because they are furthest away, they may feel invisible and not part of the conversation. You'll keep them more engaged by connecting with them. And target those actively listening to you. These individuals might smile, make eye contact, turn their body toward you, or nod.

By following the above, you'll reduce speaking anxiety, connect better with the audience, and increase the impact of your message.

Takeaway: Be prepared, practice, center yourself, and make eye contact.

> "Picture yourself in a living room having a chat
> with your friends. You would be relaxed
> and comfortable talking to them,
> the same applies when public speaking."
> — **RICHARD BRANSON**

I trust in my abilities.

Everyone experiences self-doubt. It often appears right when we're about to grow or step into something new. We think, *Can I really do this?* That question isn't a stop sign, but a signal we're on the edge of something meaningful.

Whether we're looking for a new job, a different relationship, or we aren't achieving our goals as expected, we wonder if we are good enough. Then, we question if we have what it takes to succeed. Ask:

- *What are my doubts, inner conflicts, and hesitations?*
- *What is preventing me from reaching my full potential?*
- *What fears are standing in the way of progress and growth?*
- *What is holding me back from achieving my dreams?*
- *How can I change this mindset?*
- *Why do I not have faith in myself?*

Doubt is nothing more than a product of your own thinking and a lack of self-trust. Instead of falling into this mindset, look back on everything you've already accomplished and the obstacles you've overcome. Recall how you felt after your successes and keep remembering these accomplishments to quiet the doubts.

Trust in yourself and what you can do.

Takeaway: Believe in your potential.

> "I used to doubt my ability and what I was capable of,
> and then I changed my mindset.
> It made me a better person, a better advocate,
> and opened doors for me to help instigate real change."
> — DYLAN ALCOTT

I rise above my doubt, leaving the nagging whispers behind.

Imagine if the Wright Brothers had questioned their dreams of flying. What if they listened to the skeptics who doubted the plane's ability to fly? The world may have never experienced the thrill of flight.

As J.M. Barrie said, "The moment you doubt whether you can fly, you cease for ever to be able to do it."

Doubt limits innovation and future potential. It's through the power of imagination, creative problem-solving, visualizing success, and taking decisive action that we transform fear and ascend to new heights. The Wright brothers teach us this lesson. It's in the doing that we silence doubt.

Takeaway: Silence the internal negativity and rise above the doubt.

> "The only limit to our realization of tomorrow
> will be our doubts of today."
> — FRANKLIN D. ROOSEVELT

I embrace my power.

In the wonderful movie, *The Wizard of Oz*, Glinda told Dorothy that she always had the power to leave the Land of Oz and return to Kansas. Dorothy was afraid. How many of us possess the ability to change our circumstances, to progress in life, and to seize opportunities, yet we let fear hold us back?

Channel your worries and use them as a source of strength. Say, *My fear reminds me of what is important to me and by reconnecting with what I want, my doubts lose their power.*

Roy T. Bennett once said, "Instead of worrying about what you cannot control, shift your energy to what you can create."

You have more power than you think. It's time to believe in it and unleash your potential.

Takeaway: The power lies within you.

> "You've always had the power my dear,
> you just had to learn it for yourself."
>
> **— GLINDA THE GOOD WITCH, *THE WIZARD OF OZ***

Focus

Give Your Attention to What You Want

Your mindset is the lens through which you see life.
Shift your focus and your reality begins to shift, too.

My mindset
creates my reality.

What you focus on, you see more of. It's that simple. Have you ever noticed that when you get a new car, you see more of that same model on the road? What you give your attention to is what you notice.

What occupies your thoughts? Where do you place your focus? Abundance or lack, success or failure, problems or solutions, positive or negative? Your reality is a product of your mindset. Want a different reality? Then, revise your focus.

Shift your attention and you'll change what you experience.

Takeaway: What you focus on grows. Direct your energy toward what you want, not what you don't.

"What we see depends mainly on what we look for."

— JOHN LUBBOCK

I have the ability to shift my perspective.

The way we view events and situations influences not only our feelings and actions, but also our reality. This shapes our mental state, which directly impacts our well-being. Remaining mindful of our perceptions can help improve our lives.

Picture this: Two individuals plan a beach getaway and face rain on their arrival.

Person One's perspective is:
- *This rain is ruining my vacation.*
- *Why does this always happen to me?*

Person Two's point of view is:
- *Since it's raining, I'll go see that movie I've been wanting to watch.*
- *This is out of my control, so I'll make the best of it.*

You can improve your life by changing your focus and thinking. Is your outlook currently positive or negative?

Your mindset and perspective are the architects of your reality. If you don't like what you're building, you can construct something different. When you do, you can create a new outcome.

Takeaway: Confucius said, "You are what you think."

> "It isn't what you have, or who you are,
> or where you are, or what you are doing
> that makes you happy or unhappy.
> It is what you think about."
>
> — DALE CARNEGIE

It's in my best interest to pause before reacting.

Often, it's beneficial to pause and assess a situation or conversation before we react. This gives us a moment to process, then decide on the best route to take.

Sometimes I speak before processing what the other person is trying to say. I'm too busy crafting a response to listen. My intentions can be good, yet the outcome isn't always ideal. I've discovered that if I slow down, pay attention, and listen, then take a pause before speaking, it creates a better outcome for all.

There's an internal need to respond right away, though we don't need to react immediately. Instead, take a breath or say, "I'll think about it and get back to you later." This allows time to reflect before responding. Initially, the silence may be uncomfortable. However, this extra time will refine your message for a more favorable result.

Takeaway: Pause. Evaluate. Respond.

"Think before you act; think twice before you speak."
— THOMAS BROWNE

Tuning into my thoughts
makes me more aware of myself.

Each of us possess an inner compass—a blend of feelings, emotions, and thoughts—that steers our focus. If negativity seems to take over our mental state, it may be a sign that we're overthinking and too much in our heads. This causes unnecessary stress, anxiety, fear, and other emotions that block our growth and happiness.

Mindset and feelings are interconnected and influence each other. But negativity isn't always bad. It kicks in our survival mode and protects us from making wrong decisions, too. The question we have to ask ourselves is if it's helping or hindering us from what we want to do.

It's not the thought itself that holds us back, but the meaning we give it.

Takeaway: Tune in and question your thoughts.

"The direction of the mind
is more important than its progress."
— JOSEPH JOUBERT

I don't let my thoughts or distractions overwhelm me.

Monkey mind is a Buddhist concept that refers to the lack of control over one's chaotic thoughts.[29] Similar to a monkey swinging between branches, our attention shifts rapidly and sometimes erratically as thoughts pop in and out of the mind.

For example, I may have a thought to fix dinner, but if I keep writing instead, then another one will mysteriously appear, like remembering that I need to take out the garbage. It continues on and on. The mind never seems to take a break.

However, a thought is just a thought and means nothing unless we give it meaning. And it's still just a thought until we act on it.

Takeaway: Thoughts are temporary.

"Learn any form of meditation.
Spend twenty minutes every day, if possible,
in meditation, listening to the crazy monkey mind
inside you, and learning how to still the thoughts
and discover that big, deep soulful part of yourself."

— ELIZABETH LESSER

My thoughts have no power unless I give them meaning.

A challenge may arise when we begin to analyze our thoughts. There's a fine line between analyzing and ruminating.

In analyzing, there's an objective or a goal we're working toward.

Rumination is a mental loop that's commonly negative, based on past events or future what-ifs. It can rapidly gain momentum and trigger a cascade of thoughts, quickly escalating into a spiral. We think, *Why did I say that?* or *This is not important, so why am I still worrying about it?* The thinking train continues to pick up speed until something stops it in its tracks.

Create moments of refuge throughout your day, whether through a quick meditation or journaling, to release mental spirals, refocus, and gain clarity. These tools help you to tune into your inner voice, prioritizing your desires over mental chatter.

If you encounter monkey mind, try:
- Taking a few deep breaths or practicing meditation to quiet the thoughts.

- Creating a gratitude practice and looking for the good in your life.
- Participating in a mindful action, like gardening, cooking, painting, or cleaning.
- Replacing it with something you want to focus on or repeating a positive affirmation.
- Looking at the thought as a cloud floating through your mind and moving on instead of trying to fight it.

Finally, if negative thoughts consistently interfere with daily life, consider talking to a therapist or mental health professional. They can be a guide and provide tools to help you.

Takeaway: A thought means nothing unless we believe in it.

"A thought is harmless unless we believe it.
It's not our thoughts, but our attachment
to our thoughts, that causes suffering.
Attaching to a thought means believing that it's true,
without inquiring. A belief is a thought
that we've been attaching to, often for years."
— BYRON KATIE

I'm mindful of how I spend my time.

Many daily decisions, like doing the dishes, are made automatically. We operate on autopilot without needing to think through every move, which can be helpful. However, this sometimes has a downside. By choosing the same behaviors, actions, and emotions, we get the same results.

"Autopilot is a growing problem. It is becoming our default mode of operating, whereby we are sleep-walking into our choices. Making unconscious, automatic decisions to help with certain routine tasks is an evolutionary mechanism that has developed to stop our brains from overloading. Yet today, making choices on autopilot has seeped into more areas of our lives and relationships, causing us to feel out of control," states Mark Williamson, PhD, Director, Action for Happiness.[30]

When we're more conscious of our actions, we can change our habits and intentionally use our time to shape a more gratifying life. The first step is to become aware of our autopilot types.

Here's a summary of each:[31]
- The Pleasers: Those who say yes to everything to please others. This can lead to resentment and keeps them from focusing on what is important to them.

- The Pacers: This type tries to pack in as much as possible. They're too busy doing rather than being. (This is me.)
- The Passengers: People in this category are overwhelmed with choice and information. They let the world dictate their choices and follow the crowd too often.

If you fall into the category of a pleaser, learn to say no and cancel unnecessary engagements. If you're a pacer, do what's important to you first and have a bedtime routine to make sure you get the rest you need. For the passengers, do something new to break out of autopilot and prioritize your to-do list by working on your top three tasks.

"People recognise that the choices they are making don't add up to the life they want to live. We can all do better at living more purposefully. The opposite of autopilot is purposeful living."[32]

Takeaway: Pay closer attention to your choices.

"Once we've become aware of our own individual autopilot behaviours, we can start to change them. We can turn our passive and unconscious habits into active and positive ones. This will allow us to reconnect with what really matters."

— DR. MARK WILLIAMSON

I cut out distractions,
so I can focus on what's important.

It's easy to get distracted when there's so much external noise—media, ads, emails, texts, and notifications.

Thoughts move in and out, some of them so sudden, or even bizarre, that we wonder where they came from. Maybe something externally prompted them to appear. For example, if I'm checking my email and I see an ad for coffee, I may think about having a cup of coffee instead of concentrating on my inbox. Even as I write this, I just saw the water glass next to me and all of a sudden I'm thirsty. I wasn't a few seconds ago, but now I am. See how easy it is to get distracted.

To lessen distractions:
- Silence your phone.
- Close the email tab.
- Turn off notifications.
- Declutter your workspace.
- Schedule time to check your devices and set a limit, such as 15-30 minutes after lunch before you get back to work.

When you silence the external noise and eliminate the visual clutter, you'll find your focus sharpens and output improves.

Takeaway: Silence the external noise.

> "One way to boost our will power and focus
> is to manage our distractions
> instead of letting them manage us."
> — DANIEL GOLEMAN

My productivity improves when I focus on a single task.

We all try to multitask, but are we really doing it? Yes, we may be able to multitask on simple actions, like doing chores while listening to music or talking on the phone. Even then, we can miss something. For more complex tasks, what we are really doing is just switching back and forth from one task to another. We're not working on both at the same time.

In today's fast-paced electronic environment, we're so distracted that it makes it hard to concentrate on just one thing. Gloria Mark, a Professor in the Department of Informatics at the University of California, Irvine studied task switching. She discovered that people switch tasks, meaning they get interrupted or change their focus, every three to ten and half minutes, depending on the task or project.[33] She continues, "When people are switching contexts every 10 and half minutes they can't possibly be thinking deeply. There's no way people can achieve flow." Talk about a productivity waster.

I still fall into this trap. I'll be watching television and decide to check my email at the same time. All that happens is that I have to rewind or pause the show because my concentration switched over to my emails. This creates tension and a feeling of being overwhelmed. Too much stress leaves me overloaded and I can't accomplish anything.

"Multitasking may seem efficient on the surface but may actually take more time in the end and involve more error," states psychology professor, David Meyer. "Even brief mental blocks created by shifting between tasks can cost as much as 40 percent of someone's productive time."[34]

Instead, we should concentrate on one task at a time. This is how we take our best shot. It not only increases productivity, but also helps us get into flow state or the zone where we accomplish so much more.

Takeaway: To achieve peak performance, focus on one thing at a time.

> "From the neck up is where you win
> or lose the battle. It's the art of war. You have to
> lock yourself in and strategise your mindset.
> That's why boxers go to training camps:
> to shut down the noise and really zone in."
> — ANTHONY JOSHUA

My flow state
requires singular focus.

When we concentrate on one thing, we more easily fall into the zone where all distractions seem to fade into the background and ideas flow naturally. Time becomes irrelevant and loses its importance.

Purposely direct your attention toward your desire. Focus fully on it. In this space, you're better at your craft, feeling more confident and at peace. This is where creativity flourishes, we accomplish the most, and become aligned with our true selves.

Takeaway: Everything flows better when I'm in the zone.

> "Flow helps to integrate the self
> because in that state of deep concentration
> consciousness is unusually well ordered.
> Thoughts, intentions, feelings, and all the senses
> are focused on the same goal. Experience is in harmony."
> — MIHÁLY CSÍKSZENTMIHÁLYI

I make a plan
outlining the steps.

A good plan with clear objectives and deadlines will ease worries about what comes next. This way you can place your attention on what's most important. An understanding of the steps involved helps to avoid confusion and indecisiveness. It's like a map; if you know where to turn, you won't get lost.

While the plan might not go exactly as expected, it offers a useful framework. Your journey may require unplanned steps. Unexpected detours can sometimes be the key to reaching your destination. So, be open to adapting.

As you focus on the goal, distractions and doubts lose their power, becoming less impactful. Instead of ruminating over the unknown, knowing the next step will allow you to have more time and energy for what truly matters in achieving your goals.

Takeaway: Map out the steps.

"I have learned over the years
that when one's mind is made up, this diminishes fear;
knowing what must be done does away with fear."

— ROSA PARKS

I batch similar tasks together for improved performance.

Task-batching involves grouping similar tasks together and working on them back-to-back in a specific time period. This helps keep our focus aimed in one direction. It's more productive and efficient, while also lowering stress and potentially boosting creativity.[35]

Many of us do this in our personal lives already, like batching several errands in one trip or meal prepping for the full week ahead on Sunday.

Here's an example of how I might batch my schedule:
- 8am - 10am: All things writing, whether it's upcoming books or newsletters
- 10am - 10:15am: Break
- 10:15am - 12pm: Marketing including filming videos, designing graphics, and other content creation
- 12pm - 1pm: Rest with lunch, meditation, and/or movement
- 1pm - 3pm: Meetings
- 3pm - 3:15pm: Break
- 3:15pm -5pm: Communication like emails, social media comments, etc.

Prioritize your schedule and tackle the most important tasks first thing in the morning. This way if the day takes an unexpected turn, goes off-track, or you simply don't have enough time to finish the assignment, then at least you'll have made progress on your top priorities.

You can batch similar activities not only by time, but also by day. For instance in my schedule, Mondays could be for writing, Wednesdays for meetings, and Fridays for planning and content creation.

Each day's schedule may look different depending on your duties. For large projects, break them down into smaller tasks you can accomplish in an allocated time block.

Takeaway: Batching similar tasks saves time, boosts focus, and reduces stress.

> "The key is not to prioritize what's on your schedule but to schedule your priorities."
> — STEPHEN COVEY

My creativity sparks when I innovate.

We've all experienced getting stuck on a project. When Thomas Edison got stuck on a problem, he would nap in a chair while holding a small steel ball. As he fell asleep, his muscles would relax and the ball would drop, waking him up. He stated, "Great ideas originate in the muscles." Maybe he was on to something. But does it work?

Scientists have repeated this technique and found it does. "People following his recipe tripled their chances of solving a math problem. The trick was to wake up in the transition between sleep and wakefulness, just before deep sleep."[36] There's a sweet spot. "It is a small window which can disappear if you wake up too early or sleep too deep," says Delphine Oudiette, a sleep researcher at Paris Brain Institute.[37]

If you feel stuck, try to relax by napping. Let your imagination run wild. It could spark a brilliant new idea.

Takeaway: Be inventive, explore creative solutions, and think differently.

> "I never did a day's work in my life. It was all fun."
>
> — THOMAS EDISON

I find win-win solutions by understanding both sides.

Sitting in a local coffee shop, I observed a small dispute between a customer and the barista. The drink didn't fill the cup, so the barista wanted to make a new one. The customer insisted it was fine and the barista responded, "No problem, I can easily make another one." After a few rounds of this back-and-forth debate, the barista said, "I'm already making it."

Watching the events unfold, I attempted to understand the situation from the viewpoint of each person. Maybe the barista wanted to ensure the customer felt their purchase was worthwhile. Maybe the customer didn't want to bother the barista, hold up the line, or was content with the order.

Finally, the barista handed him both drinks and the customer said, "Today is my son's birthday, so I will give him this one." By taking a step back and looking at the bigger picture, we find that not only did the barista feel better by supplying the customer with top-notch service, but also the customer got to celebrate his son a little extra with a surprise coffee.

When you are in a situation, put yourself in the other person's shoes. Take a step back and rethink the event. This will bring more clarity and understanding to help find a win-win.

Takeaway: Understanding all sides leads to better outcomes for all.

> "The greatest tragedy for any human being
> is going through their entire lives believing
> the only perspective that matters is their own."
>
> — DOUG BALDWIN

Every day I get to choose between optimism and pessimism.

Our perspective is like a camera lens. What we choose to focus on becomes our entire frame, but sometimes clarity comes when we zoom out and see the whole scene.

We are all familiar with individuals who have experienced car accidents, divorces, illnesses, or significant setbacks. But each person has a unique outlook. What causes them to perceive the same event in different ways?

The event's true impact depends on where we place our focus and from which angle we choose to perceive it. To some, it's terrible. To others, it's not as bad as it could have been. Same situation, different response.

The optimist, using a wide-angle lens, sees a bigger picture rich in lessons, while the pessimist, zoomed in on a single detail, might miss out on the full scale of opportunities. It's the same as looking at a picture of a flower field. If we only focus on one flower, we don't see the panoramic view.

Alternatively, we could apply a different filter, like seeing through someone else's eyes. A new perspective might reveal something we hadn't even considered.

Takeaway: Change the lens, refocus, and widen your perspective to see more opportunities.

> "The optimist sees the donut,
> the pessimist sees the hole."
>
> — OSCAR WILDE

CHAPTER 4

Beliefs

Challenge Your Perspective and Question Your Reality

What we believe directly influences
how we view situations
and this ultimately shapes our lives.

Evaluating my beliefs helps me to refine and improve them.

We have countless random thoughts daily, yet thinking them doesn't validate their truth. A thought becomes a belief when we accept it as truth, especially if it's repeated.

"Beliefs create a cognitive lens through which you interpret the events of your world and this lens serves as a selective filter through which you sift the environment for evidence that matches up with what you believe to be true," states psychologist, Jennice Valhauer.[38] So, if you believe it's going to be a difficult day, then you'll look for proof that it is by finding information to back up this belief. For example, you'll be more fixated on hitting all the red lights if you're expecting signs for a bad experience.

Valhauer continues, "When the brain is primed by a certain belief to look for something, it shuts down competing neural networks, so you actually have a hard time seeing evidence to the contrary of an already existing belief. That's why people who are depressed see a more depressing world. It's also why you are so convinced that your view of the world is the 'truth.'"[39]

Remember, our focus shapes our thinking, our thinking creates our beliefs, and our beliefs form our reality.

Are there any beliefs that are holding you back and undermining your life? If so, it's time for a revision.

Takeaway: A belief is a just a thought we consider to be true.

> "Whether you think you can or think you can't,
> either way you are right."
>
> — HENRY FORD

I examine and sift through my beliefs for accuracy.

We use our belief systems to define and justify everything, which nurtures our egos. The deeper we believe in something, the more resistant we become to differing perspectives. Our egos want to be right. Yet, this type of thinking impedes growth.

Instead of blindly accepting beliefs, challenge them by asking:

- *Are my beliefs valid and based on facts?*
- *Is there more than one correct answer or viewpoint?*
- And the big question that many don't want to face, *Am I wrong?*

If we want growth, perhaps it's time to examine our viewpoints more closely and challenge our beliefs. We could be defending and trying to prove something that is inaccurate.

Takeaway: We perceive events through the lens of our own experiences.

"You will always define events in a manner which will validate your agreement with reality."

— STEVE MARABOLI

What I believe is true becomes my reality.

The placebo effect demonstrates the incredible power of our beliefs. It's where one group takes a medication and the other group is given a placebo, or a sugar pill.

Dr. Jacob Towery, a psychiatrist and Stanford University professor, states, "Regardless of the disease or condition, about 30-40% of people can have significant improvement in their symptoms even when taking a placebo (sugar) pill, if they believe that the pill is going to be helpful."[40] This shows that our beliefs solidify, validate, and reinforce our reality.

There is also the nocebo effect, which is based on a person's expectations of taking a drug.

According to Dr. Towery, "When a physician emphasizes the potential side effects of a medicine, and the patient believes they will develop those symptoms, even if given a sugar pill, these patients can develop the adverse side effects, just based on what their mind expects."[41]

Our beliefs are very influential. What we want to see and believe, manifests. Mindset is our most powerful tool. Let's use it wisely.

Takeaway: Mindset is our greatest asset.

"To a large extent,
the brain doesn't distinguish real from imaginary,
and this underpins some aspects of the placebo effect.
When you imagine that something is happening,
it really is happening as far as your brain is concerned,
and it releases the chemical substances necessary
to confirm that what you're imagining is indeed real."

— DAVID R. HAMILTON

I keep an open mind and question my beliefs.

Beliefs are hard to change. When we are presented with contradictory information, we often reject it, known as confirmation bias.

"It's the natural tendency to seek out information or interpret things in a way that supports your existing beliefs. Interacting with like-minded people and media reinforces confirmation bias. The problem with confirmation bias is that it can lead to errors in judgment because it keeps you from looking at a situation objectively from multiple angles," says Keith M. Bellizzi, a professor in the Department of Human Development and Family Sciences at the University of Connecticut.[42]

So how do we change it? Bellizzi adds:[43]
- Keep an open mind, try new things, and search out other perspectives.
- Base your opinions on accurate, objective, and verified evidence.
- Don't be swayed by outliers.
- Be wary of repetition because repeated false statements can seem more truthful.

Our beliefs are shaped by what we want to be true. If we want to become more objective, then we need to be open to different perspectives. Once we do, we see things in a new light.

Takeaway: I'm receptive to different ideas.

> "The real voyage of discovery
> consists not in seeking new lands
> but in seeing with new eyes."
> — MARCEL PROUST

I understand that my belief may not be factual.

Have you heard about the infamous invisible gorilla experiment? In this video, the audience watches people throw a ball back and forth, and are asked to note how many times those wearing a white shirt pass the ball. About halfway through, a person in a full gorilla costume walks into the game beating his chest, then leaves.[44]

Afterwards, the researchers questioned the participants. Half of them did not see the gorilla because they were so focused on following the ball. "More than that, even after the participants are told about the gorilla, they're certain they couldn't have missed it."[45] We believe what we want.

Selective attention can cause you to miss opportunities. Expand your perspective and question your assumptions. Don't be so closed-minded that you can't accept the existence of a gorilla, or other possibilities sitting in front you. Beliefs don't always align with the truth.

Takeaway: Be skeptical of your perceptions.

> "What we believe is based upon our perceptions.
> What we perceive depends upon what we look for."
>
> — GARY ZUKAV

I can alter the limiting and misleading mental illusions.

Mindset, much like magic, is riddled with unreal illusions and misconceptions. It's something we've created, not necessarily factual. Think of magicians. These fascinating performers weave together storytelling, sleight of hand, and psychology, leaving audiences questioning reality.

To illustrate, we see a magician holding a card. Then, with a flick of the wrist, the card disappears. It seems to vanish into thin air. But did it really vanish? No, it just appears that way because that's what we were primed to see. Our mindsets, similar to a magician's tricks, are full of illusions and fallacies. Once we buy into a belief, that's all we'll recognize.

Unleash your inner power by releasing limiting beliefs. Prepare to be amazed at the possibilities and reality you can create like magic once you release mindset restrictions.

Takeaway: Whether we see possibilities or limitations depends on our mindset.

> "Never say never because limits like fears
> are often just an illusion."
> — MICHAEL JORDAN

I'm becoming more aware of my habits and actions.

Often, we perform actions without thinking, completely unaware of what our brains are processing. Once we learn to do something, like walk, bike, or drive, the steps become ingrained in us. That's a good thing when we're talking about the automatic nervous system. We wouldn't want to be preoccupied with basic bodily functions such as breathing, digesting, and heartbeat.

The subconscious governs a lot of our day and influences 90-95% of our behavior.[46] "It is estimated that approximately 95% of our thoughts, feelings and memories live in our subconscious. The human brain can absorb about 11,000,000 bits of information a second, the conscious mind can only process about 40 bits a second."[47] That's a tremendous amount of information that bypasses our awareness, making where we place our focus extremely important.

Without intention, our subconscious falls back on old ways of thinking, habits, and behaviors. The more we repeat them, the more these become our default setting.

However, when we're conscious of counterproductive thinking and behaviors, we have the power to adjust and cultivate practices that are more beneficial.

As Earl Nightingale said, "Whatever we plant in our subconscious mind and nourish with repetition and emotion will one day become a reality." Let's pause and consider if our actions are habitual or intentional.

Takeaway: Everything you focus on and repeat daily becomes your life.

> "Most people don't even acknowledge
> that their subconscious mind is at play
> when the fact is it is a million times
> more powerful than the conscious mind."
> — DR. BRUCE LIPTON

I review my beliefs to encourage a growth mindset.

Repetition, often referred to as the mother of learning, is how we master any trait or skill. The more we do something, the more it gets cemented into our brain's neural pathways. Think of these pathways as highways that transmit information. The more they get used, the deeper the information gets ingrained, eventually becoming automatic.

Beliefs work the same way. A strong belief will reinforce our conviction about something until it becomes second nature. We won't even question it.

However, we should reflect on our beliefs. Some may be outdated or need to be revised. Ask, *Are they limiting or do they encourage growth?* We build what we believe, so consciously construct empowering narratives.

Takeaway: Be mindful of your beliefs.

"Repetition is the mother of learning, the father of action, which makes it the architect of accomplishment."

— ZIG ZIGLAR

I focus on the future, not the past.

When making choices, we instinctively rely on our past for direction. Sometimes it's helpful, other times it may be an unreliable reflection of reality. Our minds distort the past, similar to how rearview mirrors distort objects.

Memories are rarely exact replicas of the past. Instead, they're pieced together into stories, yet not always accurate, woven from beliefs, emotions, intuitions, guesses, and scattered fragments of recall.[48] It's like the childhood game of telephone in which your memory has "been altered with each retelling," states a Northwestern medicine study.[49]

What this means is that we are actually not remembering the event itself, but the last time we recalled it.

Furthermore, our emotions during an event usually differ from our later recollections, thus affecting our memory. "If you remember something in the context of a new environment and time, or if you are even in a different mood, your memories might integrate the new information," says Donna Bridge, a postdoctoral fellow at Northwestern University Feinberg School of Medicine.[50] Our understanding of past events might be flawed because time distorts memories.

Spend less time looking in the rearview mirror of your past and at the things that went wrong. Instead, focus on the road ahead. There is so much more to see out of the front windshield. With a simple adjustment, a whole new world of insights, opportunities, and perspectives come into view. You are in the driver's seat.

Takeaway: Objects in the rearview mirror may not be as they seem.

> "Always focus on the front windshield
> and not the review mirror."
>
> — COLIN POWELL

My life gets better by updating my outdated beliefs.

Clinging to beliefs that no longer serve us hinders new perspectives, ideas, and solutions from appearing. To achieve different results, we need to revise our beliefs. Otherwise, we'll just keep getting the same outcomes. It's time to upgrade so we can adopt a new mindset.

Here are some steps to update a confining belief:
- Challenge the belief. Is there evidence to back it up?
- Be curious and explore different ways of thinking to see if your belief is restricting.
- Reframe it to something that aligns with your inner truth.
- Take actions that help to reinforce this new belief. Action helps to anchor it.

When we release and rewrite our limiting beliefs, we then make room for more beneficial ones.

Takeaway: Improve beliefs through self-reflection.

"We question all of our beliefs,
except for the ones that we really believe in,
and those we never think to question."

— ORSON SCOTT CARD

I'm creating a new narrative for myself by revising my story of limitations.

The upholding of our beliefs, even those that are self-limiting, is a universal human tendency. One clue to see when we are defending a limitation is if we keep explaining why we can't do something or why it won't work. Defense is usually a sign the ego is attached to this limitation story.

Using statements like *I never get it right, I always mess up, It's too difficult,* or *I'm not smart enough* are self-imposed limitations that become self-fulfilling prophecies. These block us from seeing alternatives.

Brian Tracy said, "You begin to fly when you let go of self-limiting beliefs and allow your mind and aspirations to rise to greater heights."

Upgrade these beliefs by writing new ones. Then watch yourself soar.

Takeaway: Break free from your restrictions and craft a fresh narrative.

"If you fight for your limitations,
you get to keep them."

— JIM KWIK

I am the maker
of my own reality.

We make our own realities each day by what we choose to do. Consciously or unconsciously, we continue to do things because of ingrained beliefs, habits, and routines. Maybe we're scared to stop, don't know how to, or are unaware of what we're doing.

Releasing something from your life, such as a belief, a habit, a behavior, or a relationship, creates a ripple effect, immediately changing your direction and your life's trajectory. The simple act of consciously choosing to stop doing something or letting it go, no matter how small, transforms your life and opens up space for new experiences.

Takeaway: Consciously choose constructive changes.

"Change is the most beneficial power available to you, simply change the things you don't like, replacing them with your true desires."
— STEVEN REDHEAD

My actions are a result of what I expect.

Our expectations directly influence our behavior. What we expect and believe determines how we act and behave.

"People do better when more is expected of them. In education circles, this is called the Pygmalion Effect. It has been demonstrated in study after study, and the results can sometimes be quite significant. In one research project, for instance, teacher expectations of a pre-schooler's ability was a robust predictor of the child's high school GPA," states Ulrich Boser, educational advocate and researcher.[51]

It's not just what others expect of us that influences our behavior. It's also what we expect of ourselves. Our behavior is a product of our expectations and our actions are determined by what we believe will happen. Let's believe in ourselves, set our expectations for what we want, and aim.

Takeaway: My behavior is determined by my anticipations.

"My actions will follow my expectations."
— JOEL OLSTEEN

My beliefs no longer hold me captive.

Our limiting beliefs and thinking are invisible walls that confine us, while we're unaware that we hold the key to the cell. The Eagles' song, "Already Gone," began playing in my mind. It's about living life in the chains of self-imposed limitations and not realizing we have the power to escape. It's time to open the lock.

The boundaries you set for yourself are a result of your own thinking.

Sometimes we find ourselves trapped in a belief or get stuck in the mindset of *I am not capable of...* Who says so? We create our own prisons using such statements.

I once heard a metaphor about young elephants that are tied to small ropes to keep them from roaming. As calves, they tug and struggle, but can't break free. Eventually, they stop trying. As adults they could easily break free, yet they remain tethered because their beliefs say that it's impossible to escape.

How many of our own self-imposed beliefs are just like that rope? Limiting thoughts keep us stuck. It's not that we can't move forward, it's our belief that tells us we can't.

Limits block potential, whereas possibilities open doors. What is your inner voice telling you? Is it keeping you tethered or helping you to break free?

If it's not uplifting or empowering, it's time to flip the script. Don't let the past define your future. Revise your narrative. It's up to you to turn the page and create a better story.

Takeaway: Release self-imposed limitations.

"Go out and do something.
It isn't your room that's a prison, it's yourself."
— SYLVIA PLATH

To broaden my horizons, I push the boundaries of my comfort zone.

To foster personal growth, make a conscious effort to push past the beliefs of your comfort zone and tackle your fears. Stretch yourself until past boundaries are a distant memory. Then, you'll end up creating new beliefs.

Takeaway: Dare to try and trust in yourself.

> "Step so far outside your comfort zone
> that you forget how to get back."
>
> **— ANONYMOUS**

CHAPTER 5

Growth Mindset

Rewire Your Thinking to Expand Your Potential

A fixed mindset says, *This won't change.*
A growth mindset says, *It can.*

I see opportunities in every challenge.

Mindset dictates whether we perceive a situation as a challenge or an opportunity.

Someone with a fixed mindset sees challenges as impossible, so they won't try to overcome them. Rather than seeing the potential in a situation, they focus on all the reasons why something won't succeed, not realizing that achievement is within their reach.

Someone with a growth mindset views challenges as avenues to explore new possibilities. They have a unique ability to discover potential in even the most adverse situations.

Here are some tips to grow your mindset:
- Embrace curiosity in everything you do.
- Pursue learning for personal development.
- View mistakes and challenges as fuel for growth.
- Have an 'I can' attitude.
- Keep moving forward.
- Savor the wins.

A fixed mindset sees obstacles, barriers, setbacks, and impossibilities. A growth mindset sees learning lessons, knowledge, training, and opportunities.

Takeaway: Cultivate a possibilities mindset.

"In the fixed mindset, everything is
about the outcome. If you fail—or if you're not the best—
it's all been wasted. The growth mindset allows people
to value what they're doing regardless of the outcome.
They're tackling problems, charting new courses,
working on important issues. Maybe they haven't found
the cure for cancer, but the search was deeply meaningful."

— CAROL S. DWECK

Changing my thinking patterns creates different results.

In order to transform our lives, we need to alter our mindset patterns to get different outcomes. If we don't make any adjustments, we'll experience similar results. It's like replaying a song over and over again—the ending is always the same.

Same thoughts + same actions = same results.

Mindset acts like a radio. If we want to change the thought channel, we must turn the dial. It's through this action that we can switch to a different station. Hopefully one that is more beneficial and upbeat.

Takeaway: Change your thinking and actions to change your results.

"We cannot solve our problems
with the same level of thinking that created them."
— ALBERT EINSTEIN

The future holds great things when I leave the comfort zone and enter the growth zone.

Oh, doesn't the comfort zone provide a cozy feeling of security, like a warm embrace?

This familiar space feels safe because we know what to expect. However, staying in the comfort zone leads to stagnation, not growth. It's the demise of aspirations because they can't fully develop in this place.

According a Harvard blog, there are many benefits of leaving the comfort zone:[52]

- Helps Achieve Goals: By moving from the comfort zone into the growth zone, we become more productive and achieve more of our goals.
- Boosts Self-Confidence: Accomplishment increases our confidence, especially if we've worked hard and challenged ourselves. In return, this self-confidence boost gives us motivation to achieve more.
- Expands Awareness: Leaving the comfort zone provides us with an opportunity to discover new things, places, people, and interests.
- Gives Self-Agency: When we step out of our comfort zone, often we discover more about ourselves and what we want from life.

- Builds Resilience: We gain confidence because we learn how to better handle failure and setbacks, becoming more comfortable with stress and uncertainty.

Takeaway: Take one small step outside your comfort zone today.

> "You can choose courage
> or you can choose comfort.
> You cannot have both."
> **— BRENÉ BROWN**

I break my goals into small, manageable steps.

It's a common misconception that successful people often make quantum leaps, yet in reality, they are the result of many small daily actions. What may appear as an overnight success actually took years of consistent effort, dedication, and perseverance, showing up day after day, all while navigating setbacks and self-doubt.

Make your goals less daunting by dividing them into smaller tasks. Then move one step, take one action, and focus on today. Small steps build confidence, so you can make bigger moves.

Takeaway: Break it down!

"I want to see if I can. I don't know if I can. I want to find out. I want to see. I'm going to do what I always do: I'm going to break it down to its smallest form, smallest detail and go after it. Day by day, one day at a time."

— KOBE BRYANT

Experimentation leads to surprising and unexpected discoveries.

Develop a mindset that finds pleasure in exploring new experiences. Trying new things refines personal preferences and tastes. This can be with anything. For example, at your next meal, commit to trying a new cuisine or entrée.

I love trying different foods. Usually I enjoy it, but there have been times when the meal didn't match up to my anticipation. What's wrong with a little disappointment? Nothing. It just brings more clarity to what I do like. Have fun with experimenting. View it as an adventure.

Similarly to life, not every meal will meet our expectations. Wanting perfection in every situation is unrealistic. Yet, without taking risks and exploring new options, we might deprive ourselves of a wonderful culinary delight or our new favorite meal. It's like biting into a piece of chocolate expecting sweetness, only to discover a hint of bitterness adds depth to the flavor.

Takeaway: Be curious. Experiment often.

"Don't be too timid and squeamish
about your actions. All life is an experiment."
— RALPH WALDO EMERSON

I get rewards
by taking risks.

Success typically doesn't come to your front porch and knock on the door out of nowhere. At least it hasn't knocked on mine in that way. We must travel out of the comfort of our house and risk the possibility of failure to meet success where it's at. You don't need total bravery at first. Just enough to open the door and walk through.

Takeaway: Take the risk and seize the opportunity.

"You have to take risks.
We will only understand the miracle of life fully
when we allow the unexpected to happen."
— PAULO COELHO

A little stress helps my performance and assists me in achieving my goals.

Expanding your comfort zone is stressful, yet essential for personal development.

I know that when I broaden my comfort zone, I feel anxious. This can be a good thing. A little stress is similar to a shot of adrenaline. For example, a new challenge can increase my energy, sharpen my focus, and motivate me to perform better.

The Yerkes-Dodson Law, developed by two psychologists, Robert M. Yerkes and John Dillingham Dodson, states, "Performance increases as stress increases, and performance decreases as stress decreases. However, at a certain point, high levels of stress inhibit performance."[53] Like if you want to run a 5k, then walking on a treadmill isn't enough stress, but if you increase the speed too much, then it can result in injury.[54]

Find the sweet spot, the perfect balance, where you challenge yourself without wanting to give up or risking major reasons that could prevent you from achieving your goal.

View the act of exploring your horizons as something exciting, like a new adventure or a treasure hunt. Map out the direction with small, achievable steps that are a bit outside of your comfort zone, but not by too much.

You may not know what's around the corner, but the anticipation can move you forward. Stretching your comfort zone holds hidden treasures if you're brave enough to seek them.

Takeaway: A little stress can be a good thing.

> "It's not about getting out of your comfort zone
> to reach your goal. It's about widening your comfort zone
> so far that your goal fits comfortably inside.
> Once you do that, hitting your goals
> will be like hitting 3s for Steph Curry."
> — RICHIE NORTON

My persistence is vital to my success.

Most talent isn't innate; it's cultivated. Olympians aren't born with special talents. They're the outcome of years of hard work and perseverance. They've faced many obstacles, setbacks, and even physical, mental, and emotional wounds.

It's their growth mindset and ability to envision various routes to their dream that allowed them to overcome their challenges. Olympians show resilience by never quitting. This is how they make it to the games and sometimes even end up on the podium.

With each attempt, our understanding deepens of what needs to be done. We learn and hone our techniques with each win and loss, accumulating knowledge. This is only achieved through persistence.

Don't give up. You may be closer to receiving the medal than you think.

Takeaway: Persistence improves my abilities.

"Thankfully, persistence is a great substitute for talent."

— STEVEN MARTIN

I accept others as they are.

Acknowledge and appreciate the diverse tapestry of personalities around you. Value their special talents and embrace their individuality.

A team of identical players would never win. It's the unique skill set of each person that leads a squad to success.

Takeaway: Respect all abilities.

"A cricket team is always made up
of 11 different individuals and you want to give them
enough flexibility to be themselves."
— ANDREW STRAUSS

I ask for one suggestion on how I can do better next time.

Often, when we ask for constructive criticism, it may not provide the valuable information we need to improve.

According to Adam Grant in *Hidden Potential,* instead of asking for feedback, ask for advice.[55] Feedback assesses past performance, while advice guides future performance. He started asking, "What's the one thing I can do better?"[56] This question gave him improved, more constructive responses.

Keep in mind that not all advice is equal. Some suggestions hold more value than others. So, sift through the findings and select the most valuable information. When listening to the person giving the advice, do so with an open heart and mind, and set your ego aside. If not, you may risk missing important information. Seeking guidance is not about flattering yourself. It's about improving future performance.

Takeaway: Quality advice elevates performance.

"Rather than dwelling on what you did wrong, advice guides you toward what you can do right."

— ADAM GRANT

Revision helps me to polish and improve myself.

Progress requires action—it's how anything gets transformed. Like in writing, we have to edit, which requires time and dedication. Revisions can take much more time than the initial writing. I know this all too well. I've had to remove sentences and even entire chapters. It's a necessary step. If the narrative isn't advancing the story or serving a purpose, then it needs to be eliminated. It's a vital part of the process.

In the revising stage, the writer delves deep into the details, shaping and polishing their work. It's the same with personal growth. We reconstruct and mold ourselves, growing stronger and wiser with each experience.

The messy middle is hard. However, it's also the place where we'll experience the most growth. Be patient and enjoy all the steps. The redrafting stage is beautiful.

Takeaway: Revision is necessary for growth.

"You might not write well every day,
but you can always edit a bad page.
You can't edit a blank page."

— JODI PICOULT

Pivoting is
always an option.

We've all had moments where we feel powerless and off-track. In these times, we can pivot and go in a different direction. If we cannot change our circumstances, we should shift our perspective. Remember, we are in charge of our own reactions.

Flexibility is key when facing challenges. When something isn't working, pivot and try plan B. Like the famous line from Ross Geller, in the sitcom, *Friends*, "Pivot!" Hopefully you're not trying to get a large couch up U-shaped stairs.

Accept that things won't always go according to plan. View changes as chances for improvement. The unexpected might just lead to better results.

Takeaway: I can adjust my course.

"You can steer yourself in any direction you choose.
You're on your own, and you know what you know.
And you are the guy who'll decide where to go."
— DR. SEUSS

A fresh start
might be the better option.

Sometimes, starting over is necessary, even though it may feel painful, challenging, and defeating. It's difficult to let go of something we've put so much time and effort into. However, a reboot may be the best option.

If we continue to push and work on something that clearly isn't effective, we'll just be spinning our wheels. The same applies to any task, plan, or goal that is not yielding results. If the system isn't working, scrap it and start from square one.

Don't get bogged down by starting over; think of it as a new beginning and a shot at something better. It shouldn't be seen as a defeat, but as a chance to create something more amazing, leading us toward a more optimal course of action.

Takeaway: Reboot your system.

"Vitality shows not only in the ability to persist
but in the ability to start over."
— F. SCOTT FITZGERALD

I create, measure, and define my own success.

A growth mindset is knowing that success lies in the journey, not the destination. Success means focusing on your own personal progress rather than comparing yourself to others. Drop the comparison gauge. It's a losing battle. The real victory is the journey of personal growth and the transformation you've made.

The true measure of success is whatever you define it to be. For me, it's about becoming a better version of myself. I do this by continuously learning and experimenting with new activities and adventures. Your definition may be different.

Feel pride in where you are right now. You've come a long way and achieved so much already. It's time to celebrate you!

Takeaway: Create it, define it, and own it!

> "The only person you should try to be better than
> is the person you were yesterday."
>
> **— UNKNOWN**

CHAPTER 6

Self-Awareness

Define Who You Are
and What Matters Most

Use self-awareness as your compass.
Tune into your inner voice and let it guide you
to where you are meant to be. Find that place
of peace, joy, understanding, and contentment.

I frequently pause
to check in with myself.

What is self-awareness? It's turning inward to notice your feelings, emotions, mindset, and actions, then evaluating yourself objectively to see whether you're living in accordance with your core values.

According to organizational psychologist, Dr. Tasha Eurich, "Having self-awareness… means fully knowing who you are—your values, passions, goals, personality, strengths and weaknesses—and understanding how others perceive you."[57] She continues, "Almost everyone thinks they're self-aware but only about 10-15 percent of people have achieved the status."[58]

The development of self-awareness starts early. "By around 18 months, many children can recognize themselves in mirrors, indicating a budding self-awareness. As individuals mature, experiences and reflections further shape their self-perception."[59] Self-awareness is a product of your thoughts, actions, and life experiences.

And we can use this for personal development. Self-awareness fuels self-examination, which leads to self-improvement, revealing areas for growth.

Self-awareness → Self-examination → Self-improvement.

Take a moment to check in with yourself and objectively assess what's really going on. This helps you to better align with your true self and desires. You can't fix what you're not aware of.

Takeaway: Self-awareness is vital for self-improvement.

"Until you take the journey of self-reflection,
it is almost impossible to grow or learn in life."

— IYANLA VANZANT

My behavior
reflects my values.

To discover your core values, first, you have to make a list of what's important to you, such your passions, self-care, relationships, or work. Then, examine if your thoughts and actions are aligning with these.

Daily demands can distract you from matching your actions with your principles. When they don't add up, it creates stress and internal disconnect. To live your core values, Dr. Tasha Eurich offers these suggestions:[60]

1. Identify your core values, such as family, health, love, service, adventure, simplicity, challenge, knowledge, etc.
2. Pinpoint and focus on the most important.
3. Check in. Ask yourself, *Did my behavior align with my core values this week?*

If the answer to number three is no, what can you do next week to align your behavior with your core values? Don't try to do everything at once, or you might get overwhelmed. Go slow and pick one or two things to work on. It's not a race; it's a personal journey.

Lastly, please don't let others define your values or worth. Create your own definition. Otherwise, you'll lack authenticity, wholeness, and peace.

Takeaway: Live your own core values.

"Your value doesn't decrease based on someone's inability to see your worth."
— ZIG ZIGLAR

I value both my strengths and my weaknesses.

People who are self-aware have a better understanding of their strengths and weaknesses. However, weaknesses can be viewed as assets. They illuminate a path to improvement, highlighting specific aspects that may need attention.

If you want to discover your strengths, identify areas in your life where you excel with ease, feel more self-assured, or beam with confidence. Now, note areas that you feel unsure of, struggle in, or find difficult.

For example, maybe you excel in verbal communication, but written is more challenging. Maybe you're more comfortable talking one-on-one instead of in a group. I want you to know that not all weaknesses need to be changed. I'm okay that I don't have the skills to do certain things, nor would I want to. This information just helps to clarify the skills and areas where you might want to improve.

Another method in discovering your strengths and weaknesses is to consider your likes and dislikes. What you enjoy could be your strengths, whereas areas you avoid may be your weaknesses. A trusted friend or colleague can offer insights, some of which you may not see.

It's possible to transform a weakness into a strength. Some of the most challenging obstacles, once you overcome them, can become your best assets. As Drew Barrymore said, "Life is very interesting… in the end, some of your greatest pains become your greatest strengths."

We all have our own unique blends of strengths and weaknesses. Their inherent value is neutral. They're not good or bad, but simply aspects of ourselves. Their positive or negative effects only depend on how we define and make use of them.

Takeaway: Embrace your unique skillset.

"Self-awareness is the ability to take an honest look
at your life without any attachment
to it being right or wrong, good or bad."
— DEBBIE FORD

I'm mindful of my actions and my judgments.

There are two types of self-awareness: private and public.

Private awareness is what's going on inside of us, such as our emotions, beliefs, and thoughts. It's challenging to judge this, particularly when we shy away from examining our feelings. Sometimes it's easier and less painful not to. However, hiding or not acknowledging them won't help us to change or evolve. It's like looking into a mirror. Do we see ourselves clearly? Our visibility may be good or foggy.

Public awareness is how others see us, which may not align with how we see ourselves. The question is whether our interpretations of their perceptions of us is accurate. Similar to looking through eyeglasses, the view may be clear or distorted.

Often, the things that bother us the most about other people are reflections of our own insecurities and shortcomings. When others' actions bother us, we should reflect on whether we're also guilty of similar behaviors. I've noticed this in myself. By pausing and reflecting before reacting, we might help tweak our own unconscious actions.

Takeaway: Be mindful of perceptions, both public and private.

> "Everything that irritates us about others
> can lead us to an understanding of ourselves."
> — CARL GUSTAV JUNG

I am not defined
by the roles I play.

We get attached to the self-defined labels we use and they can become our identity. But these are roles, not who we are—we are so much more. I'm a mother, sister, daughter, friend, author, and the list goes on. Still, all of these don't describe who I am. My values and character help to describe me, such as I am kind, compassionate, loving, honest, fair, resilient, curious, creative, and joyful.

It's easy to hide behind our labels and mask our true identities. We can become so invested in them that we lose sight of ourselves. Trust me: been there, done that. When we always prioritize others first, our desires take a backseat. It's time to get in the driver's seat and steer our own lives.

Consider the effects these roles play on your well-being. Were you taught to believe you have to act a certain way or are the roles based on societal expectations? Do you feel fulfilled or trapped by them? Do they support or undermine you and your desires? Reframe and update the labels to better reflect your true self.

Throughout the years, all of us have worn many hats. However, we don't have to keep doing things the same old way. For example, as our children grow up, our roles as parents change; a baby has different needs than a teenager.

Just as it's natural for a snake to shed its skin, it's healthy for us to revise our narratives as we evolve.

Takeaway: I am so much more than the roles I play.

"When I discover who I am, I'll be free."
— RALPH ELLISON

I explore the root causes behind my motivation.

Self-awareness increases when you understand why you do something. Let's take food for example. There have been times that I've found myself mindlessly eating. I have to ask myself, *Do I want to eat because I'm hungry or is it because I'm stressed, bored, or lonely?* I've answered yes to all of the above.

Understanding the motivation behind your intention helps bring clarity to your actions and thoughts. Without it, you might see temporary changes, however, the effects will soon fade. I myself have lost weight only to regain it because I didn't have a clear why.

We can't have long-term change without understanding. Knowing our why enables real progress.

Takeaway: Know your motivation.

> "If we want to feel an undying passion for our work, if we want to feel we are contributing to something bigger than ourselves, we all need to know our WHY."
>
> — SIMON SINEK

Self-awareness fuels my improvement and progress.

Through self-awareness, we discover beliefs and thought patterns that we no longer need. The first step toward improvement is awareness. It helps to guide us in releasing limiting beliefs, destructive thoughts, and negativity. This allows for the development of new beliefs, more constructive self-talk, and a positive outlook. Even small changes can create a significant and noticeable impact.

When trying to pinpoint areas that could use a revision, ask yourself the following questions:

- *Do my beliefs support or block my progress?*
- *Does my outlook improve or worsen the situation?*
- *Do I have a positive or negative opinion of myself?*
- *Is my self-talk constructive or destructive?*
- *Do my thoughts help me or are they the source of anxiety and stress?*

If the responses lean toward the latter options, how might they be improved? Do you find yourself thinking thoughts such as *I can't, It's impossible, It won't work, There is no hope,* or *I'm not good enough*? These self-doubting thoughts arise in everyone. Change is possible.

By revising our mindsets and rewriting unhelpful dialogues, we can improve our relationships, mental and emotional well-being, confidence levels, and other facets of life. It's about becoming aware and more conscious of our inner workings. Self-awareness enables better choices.

Takeaway: Be mindful of your internal monologue.

"Awareness is the greatest agent for change."
— ECKHART TOLLE

I replace negative self-talk with more empowering inner dialogue.

Understanding our inner dialogue, that voice in our heads that continuously talks, has a great impact on our self-worth and how we live our lives. Whether we are aware of it or not, it's always in the background chatting away.

Naturally, we can't pay attention to it all the time. Otherwise, we wouldn't get anything else done. Take a few moments each day to tune into the internal conversationalist. Is it helping or hindering your progress? If it's the latter, rephrase the internal dialogue to something more beneficial.

Because our inner dialogue shapes our beliefs, we need to give it attention. What is it trying to convey? Negative self-talk creates limiting beliefs, which can hold us back from living our potential. While positive self-talk makes us feel more capable, so we persevere. Our beliefs and mental conversations are influential in shaping our lives, so it's important to prioritize developing healthier inner dialogue.

Takeaway: Listen to what you're telling yourself.

"We are what we believe we are."

— C.S. LEWIS

Self-reflection is a valuable tool for personal growth.

The practice of self-reflection allows for deeper self-awareness and fosters personal growth. It helps to guide our choices. "Research shows the habit of reflection can separate extraordinary professionals from mediocre ones," states James R. Bailey and Scheherazade Rehman, contributors to Harvard Business Review.[61]

To self-reflect is to review past events objectively. The purpose is not to place blame or shame, it's to use this information constructively to move forward. Incorrect hypotheses, unmet expectations, mistakes, and frustration all lead to valuable opportunities for reflection and growth.

Reflecting is not a place for judgment. In life, we make errors, face letdowns, and deal with unexpected outcomes. When we view mistakes as valuable lessons, reflecting on what went wrong and how we can improve, we're less likely to repeat them.

Takeaway: Grow through self-reflection.

> "I think self-awareness is probably the most important thing towards being a champion."
> — BILLIE JEAN KING

I use journaling to gain self-awareness.

Journaling helps me process my experiences and understand my reactions, improving my self-awareness. Writing lets you ponder, question, and record events and emotions, offering a chance for deep reflection. Ask yourself a few of the below questions:

- *What went right today?*
- *What went wrong?*
- *What strengths did I use?*
- *Where could I improve?*
- *What lessons did I learn?*
- *How could I better respond?*
- *What emotions or feelings came up? Did today make me happy or give me a stomach ache?*
- *Why did I have these feelings?*
- *Were my expectations met or not met?*
- *What am I grateful for?*

By reflecting on your answers, you can gain a clearer understanding of your actions. This process helps you to confront aspects of yourself or emotions you might be avoiding, reveals hidden patterns, and shows areas for improvement. Moreover, it brings to light your positive qualities, strengths, blessings, and the happiness and gratitude that often go unnoticed.

Set aside time daily to journal and weekly to review your entries. New insights, fresh perspectives, unexpected connections, and overlooked information may emerge upon later examination.

Takeaway: Journaling helps me to better understand myself.

"Journal writing is a voyage to the interior."

— CHRISTINA BALDWIN

I'm learning about myself through acts of self-love and kindness.

Be kind to yourself. Don't beat yourself up when you make mistakes and falter. They're just learning tools. It's the meaning that you give to these that determine if they are beneficial or not.

Pema Chödrön said, "Compassion for others begins with kindness to ourselves." We can't give others what we first don't give ourselves. Give yourself more. You deserve to be treated better.

Self-awareness is a lifelong journey, not a destination. It all begins with self-love and kindness. It's the foundation for authentic living, greater well-being, and a healthier mindset.

Takeaway: To know yourself is to love yourself.

"Self-awareness and self-love matter.
Who we are is how we lead."
— BRENÉ BROWN

Love positively impacts my environment.

Everything improves when we approach it with love. It makes us more compassionate, patient, and empathetic, benefitting everything around us. Our outlook, mental state, surroundings, and social connections are all positively impacted.

There is no better to place to start than with self-love. How can you feel empowered if you don't give love to yourself? You can't truly offer someone something you don't have.

Take a little time each day to appreciate the wonderful person you've become. Every morning, look in the mirror and say, *I love you just as you are.* Then, give yourself a hug. You deserve to see the light and love inside you.

Don't forget to let your heart guide you. It'll point you down the right path.

Takeaway: Love makes everything better.

"When we love, we always strive to become better than we are. When we strive to become better than we are, everything around us becomes better too."

— PAULO COELHO

I engage in mindful activities to connect to my inner self.

There are many things you can do to become more self-aware. The journey begins with being present, mindful, and connecting to your inner self. First, take a couple of slow breaths with your hands positioned over your heart. Where your hands go, attention flows.

Now, examine what has your attention right now. Is your mind focused on the present, or is it in the past or future? If it's the latter, bring it back into the now. What thoughts and feelings are coming up? Jot them down. Don't judge, just write. Awareness is how we truly understand ourselves.

Self-awareness extends beyond simple reflection. Activities such as walking, meditating, or yoga are beneficial. Others may find that gardening, fishing, or cooking helps them to know themselves better. Take time each day to connect to you. This is how you create a life true to yourself.

Takeaway: Be present.

"Your visions will become clear
only when you can look into your own heart.
Who looks outside, dreams; who looks inside, awakes."

— CARL GUSTAV JUNG

By taking intentional action, I am in charge of my life.

Through self-awareness and inner reflection, we'll know the right course of action to take. If we don't connect to ourselves, we may become disoriented and choose an unsuitable route. Instead, be mindful and take intentional action by letting it come from a place of awareness and purpose.

By aligning your intentions with your values and passions, you live more authentically. The result is that you become the master of your own destiny. This brings a powerful and long-term transformation, which will redraw the boundaries of possibilities.

Takeaway: Be intentional about your choices.

> "Mastering others is strength,
> mastering yourself is true power."
> — LAO TZU

CHAPTER 7

Visualization

From Dreaming to Doing

Go after what you want
by seeing it, feeling it, and voicing it.
Since your thoughts, beliefs, awareness, and energy
determine what you receive, visualize already having it.
Remember, you manifest what you are,
not what you want.

I consistently imagine the best-case scenario.

Did you know that the mind can't tell the difference between what is real and what is imagined? Dr. Nadine Dijkstra said, "Our results suggest that, counterintuitively, there is no categorical difference between imagination and reality; instead, it is a difference in degree, not in kind."[62]

Dijkstra and other University College London researchers further discovered, "The more vividly a person imagines something, the more likely it is that they believe it's real."[63] Neuroscience shows that brain circuits for imagination and perception overlap.[64] So, since stronger mental images feel more real, it could blur the lines and distort our sense of reality.

This information is helpful for visualization. The more vivid our mental images, the more real they feel, thus helping us to either believe in and pursue our goals, or to not. All we need is the smallest belief to begin.

So, when fear pops in with worries of the worst-case scenario, try instead to re-envision that situation as its most positive outcome. You are the screenwriter of your life, so flip the script and write a new ending. The pen is in your hand.

Takeaway: Visualize the best possible outcome.

"What we think determines what we believe;
what we believe influences what we choose;
what we choose defines what we are;
and what we are attracts what we have."
— JIM ROHN

When I combine visualization with physical action, I enhance my performance.

It's been well-known in the sports community that visualization improves performance.

Ila Borders, the first female starting pitcher in men's professional baseball said, "Two things help me to be a winner. One is I try to stay on an even keel. I don't get too high or too low. Two is I do a lot of visualization. I never see a bad pitch. I always see a good one."

When you vividly imagine an action, your brain lights up as if you're really doing it. Research in sports psychology shows that combining mental imagery with physical practice greatly improves sport performance.[65] That's because visualization and physical activity use the same neural pathways, thus improving motor skills without physical strain.[66]

Play like a pro and visualize connecting with the ball, hitting the pitch, crossing the finish line, getting the touchdown, or making the goal. Then, when you combine action with your vision, you set yourself up to win. Make visualization a daily practice and watch your performance soar to new heights.

Takeaway: Practice and visualize the win.

"I have been visualizing myself every night
for the past four years standing on the podium
having the gold placed around my neck."
— MEGAN QUANN

I align my emotions and energy with my intentions.

What's your biggest aspiration? Write it down now and visualize yourself as if you already have it. Mere visualization is not enough. You also have to feel it. Picture it, feel it, then be it.

Try this visualization exercise that offers a positive approach:

- What does it look like? Do you see success, achievement, victory?
- How do you feel? Do you feel empowered, strong, capable?
- What emotions arise? Are you happy, excited, optimistic?
- What's your body posture? Are you standing straight, head up, shoulders back?
- What are you wearing? Does your attire reflect your success?

Now, hold this space and embody these feelings. Refer to this several times a day and observe the magical synchronicities that unfold. The universe responds by matching your energy. Just as a magnet attracts iron, your energy—thoughts, feelings, and actions—attracts experiences that match it.

Harness your magnetism. Today is the day to own your power and become the person who already possesses what you want.

Takeaway: Become your ideal self.

"Everything is within your power,
and your power is within you."
— **JANICE TRACHTMAN**

Manifestation is mindset in motion.

If you want to practice manifesting, and you're not sure you believe you can, you know the drill: Start small so you don't get discouraged.

Try for little wins, like catching a green light or securing a good parking spot. Then, say thank you. Gratitude is a vital part of manifesting because the more things you are grateful for, the more good you will find and attract.

There are many things you can do to help the process, such as writing out your goals, creating a vision board, saying affirmations, having a positive mindset, taking action, and gratitude journaling.

Once you believe you can manifest, you'll notice more opportunities, like lucky encounters and coincidences that solve problems or open new doors. You'll receive new ideas that seem to appear from nowhere.

Play, have fun with it, and make it a game. Then, you'll notice serendipity stepping in. You may find that success comes from the most unexpected and surprising places. Experience the magical power of a manifestation mindset. As Jim Rohn said, "It's as easy to manifest a button as it is a mansion." Start believing.

Takeaway: Mindset + motion = manifestation.

> "Your whole life is a manifestation
> of the thoughts that go on in your head."
> — LISA NICHOLS

I let things unfold naturally.

We often wrestle with life, trying to bend it to our will, instead of patiently observing its unfolding. It's like a gardener forcing a flower to bloom before its time. The result of this can be a frustrating, time-consuming struggle, leaving us exasperated and impatient. This rigid approach can backfire into unwanted circumstances.

Let go of how and when things will unfold. That's the universe's job. Your job is desire and action. Know that answers and solutions will emerge as you work. Think it, write it, visualize it, believe it, and act on it. Nothing happens without action.

Allow things to progress naturally instead of attempting to manipulate situations into your preferred outcome. It might just lead to a better result.

Takeaway: Relax and just go with it.

> "Sometimes you have to let go to see
> if there was anything worth holding onto."
> — SOCRATES

I am clear on what I want.

I've discovered ways that I can block myself from what I want to manifest. First is wanting and resisting my desires at the same time. Even if I want something, I can doubt it will appear. This creates friction and confusion because I may be clear on what I want, but I'm not clear on if I can have it. Other blocks like this include fear, limiting beliefs, and negative self-talk. This causes conflict, hindering intentions.

Second is setting rigid time limits or outcomes. I can create goals with a timeline, but the trick is to stay calm if things don't go as expected. Trying to be in complete control blocks what you're trying to manifest. We have to let go and be open to it happening when the time is right. It might even look totally different than what we originally imagined.

Garth Brook's song, "Unanswered Prayers," relates to this because it's about thinking we want something and not getting it. But as it turns out, he's grateful his prayers didn't go as planned because other gifts were on the horizon.

Be patient, keep working, and trust in the process. As Ralph Waldo Emerson said, "Once you make a decision, the universe conspires to make it happen."

Takeaway: Clarity helps to release blocks.

"Ask for what you want and be prepared to get it."

— MAYA ANGELOU

I envision a brighter future with more positive results.

It's human nature to worry things will go wrong and won't work out. I've been guilty of this myself. However, it's just a waste of time and energy on something that might not ever happen. Instead, shift your thinking and focus on more positive outcomes. Picture everything easily falling into place.

If you can't envision a positive result, then try picturing a neutral one instead. One that might not be ideal, yet isn't bad either. Anything is an improvement compared to the worst-case scenario.

As Michael J. Fox stated, "Don't spend a lot of time imagining the worst-case scenario. It rarely goes down as you imagine it will, and if by some fluke it does, you will have lived it twice."

Takeaway: Imagine a better outcome.

"If you spend time worrying
about the worst-case scenario,
take time to consider the best-case scenario
and most likely scenario too."

— DR. EMILY ANHALT

I can do this.

Keep repeating this affirmation to yourself. When you find yourself thinking, *I can't*, use the below affirmations to revise your self-talk.

- When you conceive an idea, say, *I think I can.*
- Believe that it's possible and think, *I believe I can.*
- Then, act and state, *I can do it.*

Replace *I can't* with *I can*. If that feels too far of a stretch, then say, *It's a possibility*. I believe that if it wasn't possible, it wouldn't exist in your mind. Turn your vision into a reality.

Takeaway: Conceive. Believe. Achieve.

> "Whatever the mind can conceive
> and believe, it can achieve."
>
> — NAPOLEON HILL

My reality is a product of my beliefs.

People who imagine possibilities see more possibilities. People who feel abundant receive more abundance. People who are more joyful find more things to be joyful about. Successful people have beliefs that they can achieve success.

These people aren't luckier. Their beliefs and mindsets broaden their perspective, enabling them to spot potential opportunities that others might overlook. Then, they take action on those ideas and anticipate positive outcomes. Whatever you believe, you'll create more of it.

What you attract is a reflection of your beliefs, thinking, emotions, and energy. Your intentions are like a mirror, always reflecting back to you. To attract something different, you have to *BE* something different.

Takeaway: Like attracts like.

"You don't attract what you want.
You attract what you are."

— WAYNE DYER

I boldly ask for what I want.

Jim Carrey's $10 million check story is famous. Before Jim made it big, he wrote a check to himself for "acting services rendered," giving himself five years for it to be fulfilled. It came true because he had a clear intention and worked toward it.

On *The Oprah Winfrey Show* in 1997, Jim shared that about ten years earlier, "I would visualize things coming to me that I wanted. I had nothing at that time, but it would just make me feel better. I do have these things. They are out there. I just don't have a hold of them yet." Later he said, "I wrote myself a check for $10 million and dated it Thanksgiving 1995. I put it in my wallet and kept it there and it deteriorated and deteriorated, and just before Thanksgiving 1995, I found out I was going to make $10 million on, I think it was, *Dumb and Dumber*." Oprah then said, "Visualization works if you work hard." Jim replied, "That's the thing. You can't just visualize and then go eat a sandwich."[67]

By imagining, feeling, and believing he could have it, Jim turned his internal dialogue and mindset into reality. He stated, "Our intention is everything. Nothing happens on this planet without it. Not one single thing has ever been accomplished without intention."

Takeaway: Visualize, take action, and believe it will happen.

> "So many of us choose our path
> out of fear disguised as practicality.
> What we really want seems impossibly out of reach
> so we never dare to ask the universe for it.
> I'm the proof that you can ask the universe for it."
>
> — JIM CARREY

I am the designer of my life.

Our lives are shaped by our daily choices, habits, actions, and thoughts. If we want our desires to come true, we first have to make a decision to pursue them. Then, we have to take action. Yes, opportunity may come knocking, however, opportunity will not do the work for us. That's not opportunity's job. The work is our responsibility.

When opportunities present themselves, make the choice and commit to do the work. If you don't, you may regret it later. Once a choice is made, the decisions following will determine your destiny.

Takeaway: My destiny lies within me.

> "Destiny is not a matter of chance,
> it is a matter of choice;
> it is not a thing to be waited for,
> it is a thing to be achieved."
> — WINSTON CHURCHILL

I let go of the past to make space for what's important.

It's important to recognize that not everything we experience or everyone we encounter is meant to stay in our lives for the long haul. Many things are just meant to be with us for a certain amount of time. If we want to make room for the new, we have to let go of some of the old, such as outdated beliefs, hurts, regrets, people, and other weights that are holding us back.

Release what's not working to make space for what you truly want. When considering letting something go, ask, *Does this bring me joy?* If not, it might be sign that something is no longer beneficial. Your mission is to develop, adapt, and keep moving. Make peace with the past, find joy in the present, and have hope in the future.

Takeaway: You can't get to your future if you're stuck living in the past. Look forward, not backward.

> "Truly precious memories will never vanish even if you discard the objects associated with them... No matter how wonderful things used to be, we cannot live in the past. The joy and excitement we feel here and now are more important."
>
> — MARIE KONDO

I view the world with childlike wonder.

Children naturally follow their bliss. They're curious, enthusiastic, and happy. They allow their inner guidance system to take the lead without questioning their ideas or doubting if they're realistic. They just go for it.

Have you ever experienced a sudden flash of inspiration that unexpectedly yielded great results? At first your rational mind says, *No, I can't*, or, *It's not possible*. Yet, you feel pulled to do it anyway. That's your inner guidance system.

This is your natural state of joy, love, and creativity. When you let your inner wisdom lead, life is exciting and anything is possible.

This doesn't mean you're not acting like an adult. You don't have to choose one or the other, you can be both— a grown-up who experiences life's wonders with childlike joy and enthusiasm. Rediscover and connect to your inner child.

Your personal GPS will lead you to joy, if you choose to follow it. It knows what to do. Get out of your head and into your heart. Seek curiosity and have fun.

Takeaway: Rediscover the world with a childlike wonder.

"Happiness comes from living as you need to, as you want to. As your inner voice tells you to. Happiness comes from being who you actually are instead of who you think you are supposed to be."

— SHONDA RHIMES

I shape my future.

Your future is in your hands. Let's recap the tips for creating it. First, if you desire a change, you must design it. Get very clear on what you want.

Second, vividly imagine the future, see yourself living it, and embody the emotions of already having it. Try to engage as many senses as you can. *What does it look like? What do I hear? How does it feel? What am I eating? What do I smell?* It'll give you a sneak peek into tomorrow's possibilities.

Third, it's essential to work toward it. Otherwise, you won't reach it.

Finally, visualize it daily. Repetition will increase its believability. Ask yourself:
- *Why do I want it?*
- *How would it feel to have it?*
- *What steps are necessary to get it?*

Takeaway: Visualize, commit, pursue, and believe.

> "The best way to predict your future is to create it."
> — ABRAHAM LINCOLN

CHAPTER 8

Confidence

Build Self-Worth Through Courage and Action

Confidence isn't something you are given.
It's something you build.

I believe in myself and trust in my potential.

There are those who believe that if something fails after one or two attempts, then all is lost and they give up. But this mindset is far from the truth. For example, baseball is "a game where they fail seven of 10 times and it's still considered good."[68]

The question is: Do you believe you can hit the ball, the goal, or the target? Your success hinges on believing in your own abilities. Your mindset is a crucial factor in determining your achievements and the outcome. Want something more? Then aim high and believe you can knock it out of the park.

It's time to step up to the plate and play ball. In order to win, shift your mindset, have confidence in your abilities, and confront the obstacles. Swing for the fences, crack the bat, and hit a home run. Let the games begin.

Takeaway: Batter up!

> "Hitting is fifty percent above the shoulder."
> — TED WILLIAMS

My confidence grows with each step I take.

Don't limit yourself based on what you can do now. Understanding and growth comes from the doing. This is where you expand and reach higher levels of achievement. The first and most important step is to shift your mindset and embrace the belief that you are capable and it's possible.

It's not necessary to have all the answers initially. No one does. We'll figure it out along the way. I believe that's a good thing. If we knew every step to take, where would the fun be? The thrill is in the unexpected. Life is best lived in the journey, not the destination, where we get to explore, evolve, and find what excites us.

As Eleanor Roosevelt said, "Be confident, not certain." It's okay to be wrong and make mistakes. This is how we learn and build self-assurance.

Takeaway: Just give it a shot.

"Confidence comes not from always being right
but from not fearing to be wrong."
— PETER T. MCINTYRE

I build confidence
by behaving confidently.

Remember the old saying, "Fake it 'till you make it"? Well, that applies to confidence, too. As Brian Tracy states, "Confidence is a habit that can be developed by acting as if you already had the confidence you desire to have."

You can increase it by acting self-assured. "This is similar to the adage that the physical act of smiling can trick your brain into feeling happier… If you exude confidence, even when you don't feel that way, others will treat you differently, which will boost your confidence—and thus the cycle continues," says Hannah Owens, social worker.[69]

Here are some tips to increase your confidence:
- Focus on your strengths. What do you excel in? What do you like to do? Success and happiness breed confidence.
- Stand tall, shoulders back, and maintain eye contact. Body language and posture communicate your self-assurance.
- Reflect on your past successes. If you've done it once, you can do it again.
- Revise negative stories and inner dialogue. Go easy on yourself and don't judge.
- Treat yourself with more kindness and compassion.
- Stop the comparison trap. It's a no-win situation.

- Keep telling yourself that you are capable.

By projecting confidence, eventually, you'll naturally embody it. By mimicking self-assurance behaviors, like standing tall and speaking clearly, you can cultivate genuine self-belief.

Takeaway: Acting confident creates confidence.

> "Just believe in yourself. Even if you don't, pretend that you do, and at some point, you will."
> — VENUS WILLIAMS

Good posture empowers me and improves my confidence.

Our posture, an important but underrated tip, has the ability to make us feel empowered or not. It communicates our feelings and mental state. "How many slumping CEOs have you seen? Posture affects how people perceive you. Just as someone with good posture sends nonverbal signals of energy, confidence, and health, a person with poor body posture appears uninterested, uncertain, or lethargic," says leadership consultant, Carol Kinsey Goman, Ph.D.[70]

Posture matters. Goman adds, "Research from Kellogg School of Management at Northwestern University, discovered that 'posture expansiveness,' positioning oneself in a way that opens up the body and takes up space, activated a sense of power that produced behavioral changes in a person independent of their actual rank or role in an organization. In fact, it was consistently found across three studies that posture mattered more than hierarchy in making a person think and act in a more powerful way."[71]

The way you hold yourself speaks volumes. Good posture conveys strength, authority, and self-esteem. If you find yourself hunched over, push the shoulders back, lift the chin, and straighten the spine. The shift to good posture is immediately noticeable. Your confidence rises, energy increases, mood brightens, and you feel more optimistic. Stand tall and trust in yourself.

Takeaway: Posture is personal power.

> "A good stance and posture
> reflect a proper state of mind."
> — MORIHEI UESHIBA

The more I learn, the more confident I become.

Education is empowering. When you gain knowledge and increase your skills, it makes you feel stronger and more capable. There are unlimited ways to learn. Watch a video, try a new hobby, switch up your routine, craft a new recipe, or explore a different genre.

One invaluable tool for me is reading. Whether it's fiction or non-fiction, reading is one of the simplest gateways to personal growth. I find inspiration and it reminds me of my own abilities. Rediscover your local library. They're hidden treasures.

Be an avid learner. The more you learn, the more faith you'll have in pursuing your desires.

Takeaway: Learning builds confidence.

> "Limits only exist in your mind.
> If you want, you can do so much more."
> — **TOBIAS HEINZE**

I boost my confidence by having the courage to experiment.

Courage doesn't exist in standing still—it's in facing challenges head-on. It's in navigating through fear, using difficulties to our advantage, and enduring setbacks. It requires us to experiment with new experiences, ideas, and approaches.

Having the courage to explore is a powerful confidence builder. It can highlight hidden talents we may not even realize we have. Plus, it opens up fresh possibilities. Venture out, be courageous, and try new things. It's through trial and error that we home in on our skills and desires.

Takeaway: Explore, experiment, and be adventurous.

"You'll never get bored when you try something new. There's really no limit to what you can do."

— DR. SEUSS

I become more self-assured
with each step I take.

Don't wait around for things to improve, but work to make them better. Improvement begins with you. For example, let's say you want to travel to a new country and learn the language. Begin by downloading a language app and practicing a few minutes each day, learning basic vocabulary and phrases. The more you take actions toward your goal, big or small, the more you increase trust in yourself.

Action transforms the unknown into the known. Once something becomes familiar, fear lessens. Self-confidence is built by taking a risk, an action, and a step forward. Your success will show you're more capable than you thought. Even if you don't succeed, you'll still surprise yourself that you can handle more than you thought was possible. Either way, you'll have grown. Having the courage to try, even when you're uncertain, ultimately builds confidence.

Takeaway: Take a chance.

> "Inaction breeds doubt and fear.
> Action breeds confidence and courage.
> If you want to conquer fear, do not sit home
> and think about it. Go out and get busy."
>
> **— DALE CARNEGIE**

I use positive affirmations to empower my beliefs.

One technique that helps me boost my confidence is saying positive affirmations, while visualizing and feeling that the statements are true. If you feel unsure or lack confidence at first, just keep affirming yourself. With each repetition, the feeling of possibility will grow. Repetition strengthens belief, so be mindful of your self-talk. You don't want to reinforce a discouraging belief.

When our mindsets, emotions, and beliefs come together, we can achieve great things.

Takeaway: Positive affirmations help strengthen my confidence.

"It's the repetition of affirmations that leads to belief.
And once that belief becomes a deep conviction,
things begin to happen."
— MUHAMMAD ALI

I draw confidence from my past successes.

Every success builds faith, and if you've done it before, you can do it again. If you have fear or doubt, remembering your past achievements and expecting the best can help boost your confidence levels.

We see this in the sports arena. Players who trust in their abilities perform better. "Research on the relationship between confidence and performance confirms the following: The more a player expects to achieve, the more he actually will achieve."[72]

Let's take a tip from this success playbook and follow the winning formula. Remember your previous successes and have confidence that you'll make the goal. See it, believe it, do it.

Takeaway: Expect, believe, achieve.

"The way to develop self-confidence
is to do the thing you fear and get a record
of successful experiences behind you."
— WILLIAM JENNINGS BRYAN

Believing in myself boosts confidence.

Confidence is a belief in yourself and your abilities. It boosts motivation, enhances social skills, sparks creativity, improves decision-making, and much more.

It not only shapes others' perceptions of you, it also inspires them to pursue their own goals. I know when I'm around people who trust in themselves, it makes me feel more self-assured and energized.

Here are just a few of the benefits of boosting your confidence:[73]

- It helps you develop resilience, so you bounce back from challenges.
- You'll improve performance by reducing worry and focusing more on productivity.
- Believing in your abilities allows you to approach new things with an open mind and a sense of adventure.
- Relationships are better because you'll have a deeper understanding of others and set healthy boundaries.

Self-assurance helps you to see the light at the end of the tunnel. So, climb aboard the confidence train and inspire others with your confidence. Start nurturing a positive self-image by focusing on your strengths and accomplishments. Be compassionate with your self-talk and just do your best.

Takeaway: Full steam ahead!

"Self-confidence is contagious."
— STEPHEN RICHARDS

I have a healthy level of confidence.

Overconfidence can make us appear arrogant, rude, or closed-minded. This may cause us to become defensive when trying to show others our competence or prove our points. We should be mindful to not oversell ourselves or try to force our views on others. Neither end well.

It's better to approach life with a healthy dose of confidence and a willingness to consider new ideas than to stubbornly cling to preconceived notions or beliefs.

Takeaway: Be confident, not boastful.

"Belief in yourself! Have faith in your abilities!
Without a humble but reasonable confidence
in your own powers, you cannot be successful or happy."
— NORMAN VINCENT PEALE

I build trust when my words and actions align.

To earn people's trust and confidence in you, be honest, respectful, and match your words to your actions.

Being inconsistent, dishonest, or breaching trust with gossip or betrayal can undermine your credibility and reliability.

Once trust is broken, it can be hard to regain. However, mending the relationship is possible if you take full responsibility and admit your wrongdoings. Look the person in the eye and offer a sincere, heartfelt apology. A fake or half-hearted apology won't work and may make matters worse.

One of the most important things you can do is to truly listen and give your full attention. Don't check your phone or scan the room for someone else to talk to. Be fully present. Create a comfortable and secure space for open communication, where individuals feel heard, understood, and validated in their thoughts and feelings. This is vital to healing and mending relationships. Listen with an open mind, accept responsibility for your actions, and don't make excuses.

Takeaway: Build trust by being someone others can count on.

"Trust is the glue of life. It's the most essential ingredient in effective communication. It's the foundational principle that holds all relationships."

— STEPHEN R. COVEY

I inspire people by believing in them.

Showing confidence in others uplifts them and you'll be amazed by how they rise to meet this belief. It'll give them the strength and courage to push beyond their limits and achieve more. Belief has the power to motivate and drive people forward.

By helping others, we create an upward spiral of positivity, inspiring both the giver and the receiver.

Takeaway: Have faith in others.

"We rise by lifting others."

— ROBERT INGERSOLL

My definition of success is independent of others' achievements.

We all fall into the comparison trap. We assess ourselves as better, equal to, or worse than others. Comparison can have some benefits, such as motivating us to do something we've been putting off or appreciating what we already have.

However, there is a downside if it makes us feel envious or inferior. If these detrimental thoughts take hold, they may send us spiraling down. Comparison steals our confidence and destroys our happiness. Plus, it's a no-win situation because our lives can never be exactly like someone else's, nor should we try.

We only see a part of the story when we compare ourselves to others. We don't see the whole picture. We tend to look at the successes instead of the challenges. And their wins may come with problems we wouldn't even want to deal with. It's like the adage said by Regina Brett, "If we all threw our problems in a pile and saw everyone else's, we'd grab ours back."

If you're in the comparison trap, try to remind yourself that you are unique with your own journey and timeline. You don't need to be where they are. In fact, even if they are 'ahead' of you, it doesn't mean they're happy or have a better life.

Instead, be grateful for all the things in your life, the good and the challenging, because both make you a stronger, more compassionate human. Gratitude is where you'll find happiness and confidence.

Takeaway: My success is self-defined.

> "If you compare yourself with others,
> you may become vain or bitter, for always
> there will be greater and lesser persons than yourself."
> — **MAX EHRMANN**

I don't let others' opinions interfere with my confidence.

People's words can sometimes make you feel inadequate. However, the person didn't cause these feelings, even if that was their intention, but the feelings arose from within you. Those words only landed because self-doubt let them in.

Redirect your attention toward your strengths rather than fixating on your weaknesses.

Takeaway: Don't give your power away.

> "No one can make you feel inferior without your consent."
>
> **— ELEANOR ROOSEVELT**

I drown out the cynics and the naysayers.

Make sure you focus on your vision, not the external noise. There will by doubters who try and crush your dreams. Don't let them. Cynics might say that it's impossible because of their own self-doubt or lack of imagination. It may be beyond their beliefs or comfort zone. Maybe they are afraid to lose money or they simply can't see the potential.

Whatever the reason is, don't adopt their beliefs as your own. Don't give them that power. Hold on to your dreams and let the voices of the critics fade into the background.

When you challenge comfort zones, even if only for your own personal development, you can make others insecure. They may inadvertently feel inadequate or inferior. Cozy familiarity brings a feeling of peace and protection. Anything outside of that is too scary for some.

When others lack belief, have confidence in yourself. If you've given your power away, reclaim it today. You are worthy of success.

Your intuition speaks softly. Align with it. Let the whispers of this internal voice guide you, not the external noise. Your voice is the only one that matters.

Takeaway: Trust yourself, not the cynics.

"Don't let the noise of others' opinions
drown out your own inner voice."
— **STEVE JOBS**

I am wholeheartedly dedicated to pursuing my dreams.

Follow your dreams with all your heart. Don't let self-doubt steal your courage and hold you back from taking the chance. Explore, attempt, persevere, believe, and trust. Your dreams are here for a reason.

The four qualities listed below might be key to achieving success. They were for Walt Disney.

- Curiosity: Cultivate it by approaching life with a sense of wonder and a thirst for learning.
- Confidence: Believe in yourself and your work. Then, nothing can stand in your way.
- Courage: Have the courage to venture into the unknown. Blaze your own trail.
- Constancy: Don't lose hope or give up. Persevere and stay focused on your dreams.

Our dreams deserve a shot. They may fulfill our souls.

One of the most important things we can do is to find joy in the process, the journey, the creating, and the growing. Focusing on just the outcome will not make us happy in the long run because what we are truly looking for is the feeling we receive from developing the dream, not necessarily the end result.

Takeaway: Let your dreams light the way.

"Somehow, I can't believe that there are any heights
that can't be scaled by a man who knows the secrets
of making dreams come true. This special secret,
it seems to me, can be summarized in four Cs.
They are curiosity, confidence, courage, and constancy,
and the greatest of all is confidence.
When you believe in a thing, believe in it all the way,
implicitly and unquestionable."
— **WALT DISNEY**

CHAPTER 9

Acceptance

Let Go, Pivot,
and Trust What's Next

Adversity is a part of life.
How you react to your difficulties
defines your character, shapes your story,
and determines how fully you live.

I have the power
to redirect my course.

Why do we continue to pursue something that clearly isn't working? Here are a few reasons:

- Sunk Cost: We've spent so much time on it already that we don't want to give up.
- Fear of Change: The familiar, even if it's not working, feels safe. Change is scary.
- Identity and Validation: If we give up, what does that say about us? Are we trying to prove something to others?

All of this is based on faulty logic and limiting beliefs. Repeated attempts don't always ensure success.

We need to know when it's time to pivot, take a different approach, or release it. Ask, *Have I made any progress?* or *Am I just spinning my wheels?* Albert Einstein said, "Insanity is doing the same thing over and over and expecting different results."

Sometimes we're blinded by hope, even when the evidence suggests otherwise. This prevents us from seeing the truth. In these situations, we must change or let go of what obviously isn't working. Then, we can evaluate other approaches and lines of action.

Takeaway: Adjust the plan when necessary.

"The measure of success is not
whether you have a tough problem to deal with,
but whether it's the same problem you had last year."
— JOHN FOSTER DULLES

Not everything I try is right for me.

It's frustrating when we try to do something and it doesn't work. For example, we can put all of our efforts into opening a door, yet it refuses to budge. If we take a step back and study it, we may discover the underlying reason it won't open. Perhaps we just need another approach like simply knocking, ringing the bell, returning later, or trying another door. The first step to a solution is accepting that our current actions aren't working.

Proceeding through this door may not be in our best interest. The goal is to examine the alternatives and select one for our current needs. It could be that there is another entrance or opportunity more suitable for us. Finding the correct one, the one meant for us, reveals better options.

Takeaway: Find another option.

> "Realize that if a door closed,
> it's because what was behind it wasn't meant for you."
>
> — MANDY HALE

I use questions asking 'what' to solve problems.

When something goes wrong, we tend to ask 'why' questions, when we should be asking 'what.'

Why did this happen to me? can lead to overthinking, blame, and circular reasoning, which never proves anything.

What can I learn from this? promotes insight, learning, and growth.

"The more we ask why, the more we ruminate… Instead of asking why am I unhappy, perhaps ask what upsetting situations can I avoid," states Dr. Tasha Eurich.[74] The way we frame our questions impacts our lives. For example, instead of asking, *Why do I?* reframe it to, *What can I do?* 'Why' questions are emotional, depressing, and limiting, whereas 'what' questions are logical and action-oriented, pointing toward potential.[75]

'What' questions:
- Lead to Clarity and Action: Instead of, *Why did I mess up?* ask, *What can I do differently next time?*
- Reduce Self-Judgment and Blame: *Why am I feeling like this?* implies that something is wrong with you. *What*

am I feeling right now? opens up curiosity without shame.

- Shift Mindset from Victim Mode: Asking, *Why do I always do this?* keeps you stuck in the past, whereas, *What can I do next time?* focuses on the present and future.

By asking questions using 'what' and taking action, we silence our inner critics, the little voices in our heads that scream, *I can't.* 'What' questions promote a growth mindset by focusing on problem-solving. We see possibilities. Asking, *What can I do?* is much more empowering than, *Why can't I?*

There is personal empowerment in asking 'what' questions, as they lead to taking steps to address issues.

Takeaway: Ask 'what' instead of 'why.'

"The unexamined life is not worth living."

— SOCRATES

I'm not defined by my past.

Our past doesn't need to determine our future. If we attempt something and fail, we can perceive it in two ways: either as a waste of time or as a valuable learning experience.

It's upsetting not to get the results we want. However, each stumble teaches us something, sharpens our skills, and improves the process, which leads to more successful outcomes. Setbacks can signal a need for more preparation or idea refinement. Perhaps there is a more favorable time in the future for it to be born. Let the process unfold naturally.

Failure doesn't detract from the significance of the journey. In fact, it adds to it, giving it meaning.

Takeaway: You are not your past.

"Your past doesn't determine your future.
What matters is what you're going to do
with those past experiences to start moving forward."
— ANTONIO NEVES

I am accepting of my current situation.

We can't change what has already happened; however, we can change how we view it.

Rather than mourn what could have been, acknowledge and accept what has transpired.

When we don't accept our current situation, we fight reality, thus, we fight ourselves. We have to learn to "roll with the punches" like a boxer moves to avoid the impact of a hit.

As Muhammad Ali said, "Inside of a ring or out, ain't nothing wrong with going down. It's staying down that's wrong." You don't have to like it, but acceptance makes it a lot easier to get back up.

Acceptance is power. It's not about giving up or settling for less—it's about letting go of resistance to the things we cannot change.

Acceptance isn't weakness, but a brave surrender that says, *I can get up and start again.* This allows us to see the situation for what it is and then we can respond with wisdom, peace, and clarity instead of fear. It's the starting point of real transformation.

Takeaway: Acceptance is the key to change.

"Acceptance doesn't mean resignation;
it means understanding that something is what it is
and that there's got to be a way through it."
— MICHAEL J. FOX

I am thankful
for the things in my life.

Cherish what you have instead of fixating on what's missing. Center your attention on the goodness that already exists in your life.

This includes accepting things as they are, not as you wish them to be. Acceptance isn't approval, but it's clarity and peace. You don't have to like what is, but accepting it gives you power. Acceptance moves you forward, whereas resistance keeps you stuck. When you choose peace over struggle, you free yourself to create what can be.

Like the Rolling Stones' song shares, life doesn't always give you what you want, but you might just end up with what you need.

Takeaway: Trust you'll find what you need.

> "Happiness is not having what you want,
> it is wanting what you have."
>
> — SHERYL CROW

I'm open to change and adjust my plans accordingly.

A considerable amount of time is often wasted worrying over matters beyond our control. We ruminate over being stuck in traffic or needing to detour while driving. Things happen; plans change. The problem occurs when we cling to what we expect, not what is. As Edmund Hillary once stated, "It is not the mountain we conquer but ourselves."

A better option is to focus on the present moment. This is where opportunities lie. Sometimes a random or unexpected event can work out really well. Things don't always go as planned, and that's alright. Accept the situation, go another route, and focus on what's next. There may be something better around the corner.

Takeaway: Go with the flow.

"We must be willing to let go of the life we've planned, so as to have the life that is waiting for us."
— JOSEPH CAMPBELL

When I shift my perspective and position, I see new opportunities.

Everyone experiences days where they feel like they're moving in reverse. I know firsthand how frustrating that can be. Remember, setbacks are there to help us move forward. Taking a strategic step back or saying, *I'll get back to you*, allows us time to see things from a different vantage point and get a better understanding of the bigger picture. Know that it's okay to pause, reset, and start anew.

In sports, players frequently travel backward in order to locate a teammate who is free to receive a pass. Getting the touchdown, goal, or basket often requires a calculated retreat. Sometimes, the simplest route to victory is by backing up.

Takeaway: Switch your position.

"It's not only moving that creates new starting points. Sometimes all it takes is a subtle shift in perspective, an opening of the mind, an intentional pause and reset, or a new route to start to see new options and new possibilities."

— KRISTIN ARMSTRONG

I use my mistakes as lessons to become who I aspire to be.

Priceless wisdom can be gained from mistakes, so don't spend too much time worrying about them. Falling and starting over is an important part of the process. You need to pick yourself up and try again. By taking action, we are taught what works and what doesn't. These lessons are valuable.

When reflecting on past errors, identify patterns and use those insights to create a roadmap for a more fulfilling future. This helps you to craft a life that truly aligns with what matters most to you, bringing about a greater sense of peace and accomplishment.

Once you've seen through the looking glass, you can't unsee it. There's no turning back. Because when you see what's possible, it'll change your perspective forever.

Takeaway: Don't be afraid to fall.

"You don't learn to walk by following rules. You learn by doing, and by falling over."
— RICHARD BRANSON

I accept that the middle is unpredictable, yet necessary.

Our lives can look chaotic midway through our pursuits, but this is where we find some of our greatest growth opportunities. Difficulties have a way of revealing our hidden strengths, similar to a skilled teacher guiding us toward progress.

The messy middle makes for unpredictable tunnels full of twists, turns, and dead ends. However, to arrive at the destination, we have to go through it.

Takeaway: Success is on the other side of the chaotic middle.

"In the middle of difficulty lies opportunity."

— ALBERT EINSTEIN

I value progress more than perfection.

We often prioritize the end result instead of enjoying the process. It's wonderful when we achieve our desired outcome. However, since we spend most of our time working toward the goal, we should savor the journey.

You may not reach your planned destination and that's okay. Instead, you may stumble into something better. It is the journey that gives life purpose and meaning, not the end goal.

Takeaway: Savor and appreciate the experience.

"Sometimes, when things take longer
than you thought they would, it's just a gentle reminder
from your greater self that you have more time
than you thought, and that there's a journey to enjoy."
— MIKE DOOLEY

I give my attention
to the light.

We're all trailed by shadows—baggage that we hold from our past—such as blame, shame, and regret. However, we can minimize the amount of attention we give to these.

By redirecting our focus and looking for the good in us instead of the darkness, the shadows' influence lessens. Eventually, the shadows will gradually fade if we don't give them our attention. Then, we make space for the light to enter.

Not all shadows are bad. Some lend a hand by offering insights or feedback to aid our growth. Others nudge us to trust our hearts to guide the way, which can point us to paths we wouldn't normally consider.

Learn from the shadows, then release them, and connect with your inner light.

Takeaway: Focus on the light.

> "Keep your face always toward the sunshine,
> and shadows will fall behind you."
>
> **— WALT WHITMAN**

Peace is found in accepting what we can't change.

Loss is one of the most difficult things we have to deal with. Becoming a writer was a direct result from the losses I experienced. My husband unexpectedly passed away, then just three weeks later, my home caught fire and we had to move out while it was being rebuilt. These back-to-back events crushed me. Between losing my husband and not being able to grieve in my own home, I fell into a deep depression. I didn't want to accept what had happened. Denial hit hard.

In time, I recognized I was trying to deny my present reality and this was causing me more pain. That's when I understood that a lot of our suffering comes from wishing things were different.

As Eckhart Tolle said, "The primary cause of unhappiness is never the situation but your thoughts about it."

I'm not saying that it is easy to accept things as they are, because it's not. Nor can we control our feelings like a light switch, which is not healthy long-term. However, to truly move forward, we must make peace with what's been lost, embracing the reality that life has changed and will never be the same.

Takeaway: Embrace the now.

> "Accept—then act.
> Whatever the present moment contains,
> accept it as if you had chosen it.
> Always work with it, not against it.
> Make it your friend and ally, not your enemy.
> This will miraculously transform your whole life."
>
> **— ECKHART TOLLE**

I am more than my past.

Everyone experiences dark times in their lives. It's part of the human experience. Despite facing these challenges, your past has not defeated or defined you.

Be proud of everything you've gone through and all you've overcome. These moments have shaped you into the person you are today. Maybe their purpose was to help you grow. Your most difficult moments may bury you, but they can also have the most profound impacts on your life that inspire powerful change. View them as a new beginning.

A tulip bulb buried in dark soil, struggles its way up, until it finally breaks through to feel the sun. We are similar to the bulbs when facing challenges, pushing through the darkness trying to reach the light. This upward growth proves our resilience. Tulips symbolize hope, renewal, and a fresh start. This is something we can all embrace.

Takeaway: Even in the darkest times, new beginnings emerge.

"Sometimes when you're in a dark place you think you've been buried, but you've actually been planted."
— **CHRISTINE CAINE**

I don't allow my problems to define me.

Life deals us a hand of cards. Some are aces, others are jokers. We don't always get the hand we want. It's what we do with it that counts.

The events that unfold around us don't dictate our future, rather, it's the conscious decisions we make and the actions we take that truly shape our lives.

Our path isn't determined by the hand we're dealt—the challenges, the chances, or the possibilities—it's how we actively choose to play it. Some rise to the occasion, while others let opportunities pass them by.

When you come across a problem, are you thrown off-guard because it wasn't what you expected? Are you in unfamiliar territory? Or are you stuck wishing for the cards you previously had? Many times, a better play is out there if you look for it.

Take a step back and look at all of your hand instead of throwing in the cards and quitting. Ponder multiple perspectives. Sometimes a gamble is necessary. Then, make the best move with the hand you're dealt and start betting on yourself.

Takeaway: Maximize your hand.

> "We all have problems. But it's not what happens to us, [it 's] the choices we make after."
>
> **— ELIZABETH SMART**

CHAPTER 10

Resilience

Make Your Challenges Work for You

Fall. Learn. Rise stronger.
Don't shy away from challenges, embrace them.
Push past the fear and stretch beyond your limits.
The real victory isn't just reaching the goal—
it's about who you become along the way.

The hardships I encounter motivate me to do exceptional things.

The trials we face shape our future, ourselves. They can lead us down a different path from the one we are currently on. Perhaps, that is the reason for their existence. To guide us toward a better path and version of ourselves.

Turn your hardships into power. They have a purpose. Maybe they are there to point you in a different direction. Use them to inspire and motivate you. You never know what your difficulties may create, potentially something beneficial or incredible, until you make use of them. Your destiny awaits.

Takeaway: Hardships breed greatness.

> "Hardships often prepare ordinary people for an extraordinary destiny."
> — C.S. LEWIS

Every challenge I face is an opportunity for self–discovery.

Challenges can reveal who we truly are. When we embrace our past, our flaws, and our journey, we stop seeking validation from the outside world. Sometimes, it's the struggle that awakens self-awareness.

The first step to self-discovery is introspection, an examination of your inner self. This is where you find out who you are and who you want to be. When you embrace difficulties as avenues for exploring your potential, personal development flourishes. This mindset cultivates resilience and a stronger sense of feeling capable.

I know my greatest moments of growth arose from difficult experiences. Transforming challenges into possibilities will build your character and your strength.

Takeaway: Grow by looking inward.

"Challenges make you discover things about yourself that you never really knew."
— CICELY TYSON

The challenges I come across make me stronger.

Superman actor, Christopher Reeve, truly embodied the qualities of a superhero. Despite his paralysis, caused by being thrown from his horse, he remained determined and unwavering.

"After months of grueling rehabilitation and therapy, Christopher returned home with a new purpose."[76] He refused to be held back by his disability. He established a foundation to support research, care, and cures for spinal cord injuries, becoming a champion for the cause. Following his accident, Christopher pursued careers as a film director, executive producer, and author.

It's natural to examine life-changing events because this allows us to process and make sense of them. Yet, it's unhelpful to keep ruminating on things that are beyond our control. Although we cannot change what has already happened, we have the power to change our mindset.

Christopher's courage, determination, and perseverance serve as a powerful source of inspiration for every one of us. He said, "Some people are walking around with full use of their bodies and they're more paralyzed than I am." He just radiated hope, inspiration, and possibility.

Takeaway: Don't let obstacles stop you. Find your strength.

"A hero is an ordinary individual
who finds the strength to persevere and endure
in spite of overwhelming obstacles."
— CHRISTOPHER REEVE

I build resilience by acknowledging and embracing my emotions.

True resilience is more than just pushing through. It's the ability to rebound from adversity, whereas being numb is a state of emotional detachment—we're not feeling anything. Resilience includes accepting and allowing our feelings. We should experience the emotional spectrum of hurdles and triumphs, not hide from it.

Resilience is an art form that requires patience, practice, and a willingness to adapt. We build emotional resilience through self-awareness and the ability to handle life's ups and downs, knowing that both your emotions and the situation are subject to change. This aids in nurturing optimism and hope.

We all lose our balance and tumble occasionally. Yet, when we brush off the dust, process our emotions, get back up, and carry on, we become more resilient.

Takeaway: Emotional awareness builds resilience.

"Resilience is very different than being numb. Resilience means you experience, you feel, you fail, you hurt. You fall. But you keep going."

— YASMIN MOGAHED

Adversity may test me, but I stick with it, building my strength and grit.

I met a person whose husband was laid off due to cutbacks. Although initially upset, he took advantage of this time by enrolling in classes and broadening his skill set. After eight months, the same company rehired him, this time in a higher position, and he began earning three times his previous salary. He transformed this difficult situation into an opportunity for personal growth. This person has what I would call grit.

"To be gritty is to resist complacency. 'Whatever it takes, I want to improve!' is a refrain of all paragons of grit, no matter their particular interest, and no matter how excellent they already are," states Angela Duckworth, psychologist and author of *Grit*.

The American Psychological Association defines grit as, "A personality trait characterized by perseverance and passion for achieving long-term goals. Grit entails working strenuously to overcome challenges and maintaining effort and interest over time despite failures, adversities, and plateaus in progress. Recent studies suggest this trait may be more relevant than intelligence in determining a person's high achievement. For example, grit may be particularly important to accomplishing an especially complex task when there is a strong temptation to give up altogether."[77]

When you persevere, you build resilience to handle what life throws at you. Then, personal success makes an appearance.

Takeaway: Adversity doesn't stop me.

> "Many of us, it seems, quit what we start far too early and far too often. Even more than the effort a gritty person puts in on a single day, what matters is that they wake up the next day, and the next, ready to get on that treadmill and keep going."
> — ANGELA DUCKWORTH

I solve problems creatively and find alternative solutions.

No matter how difficult the problem, there's another way, an alternative path to explore. Even when faced with what seems to be an impossible obstacle, solutions do exist, although they might not be where you expected. Sometimes they're found in a unique approach, a new perspective, or a different mindset.

We gain resilience by facing difficulties, enabling us to recover and come back even stronger. Think outside the box and devise innovative solutions to challenges.

Takeaway: Be a creative problem-solver.

"If your only tool is a hammer
then every problem looks like a nail."
— ABRAHAM MASLOW

I can navigate
life's potholes.

Don't let obstacles discourage you. If you experience a flat tire or a warning light on the dashboard, pull over and assess the situation, then readjust. The road of resilience is a rocky journey, filled with potholes, speed bumps, detours, and wrong turns that can slow you down.

Consider obstacles as guides that move you toward personal growth and encourage you to become the best version of yourself. Be brave and step on the gas pedal instead of relying on the comfort zone of cruise control.

When the road gets rough, find a more optimal lane or route. Sometimes, all you need to do is to switch lanes for a smoother ride. If required, pause and reevaluate your direction. Then, decide on a new course of action. You just may find that the expressway is open.

Takeaway: Resilience is a road full of unexpected twists and turns.

> "If you can find a path with no obstacles,
> it probably doesn't lead anywhere."
>
> — FRANK CLARK

I keep my balance
by moving.

A bicycle is also a good analogy for life. Sometimes you effortlessly glide down the road, enjoying every moment. Other times, you brake hard or fall down. Get up and keep pedaling to propel yourself onwards.

The world is a playground just waiting for you to explore. Go out, have fun, and enjoy the ride.

Takeaway: Ride on!

"Life is like riding a bicycle.
To keep your balance, you must keep moving."

— ALBERT EINSTEIN

Hope is a tool
I use to build resilience.

Even in challenging circumstances, optimism empowers us to find hope, illuminating the path forward. We believe in our ability to uncover a solution and the motivation to push ahead. This ultimately leads to growth or greater success because we choose to not give up.

This Wayne Dyer quote resonates with me as one of his most powerful messages as he shares, "What is hope but a feeling of optimism, a thought that says things will improve, it won't always be bleak, there's a way to rise above the present circumstances. Hope is an internal awareness that you do not have to suffer forever and that somehow, somewhere there is a remedy for despair that you will come upon if you can only maintain this expectancy in your heart." Well said, Dr. Dyer.

Don't lose hope. Better things are ahead.

Takeaway: Keep the faith.

> "Optimism is the faith that leads to achievement. Nothing can be done without hope and confidence."
>
> — HELEN KELLER

I don't give up, even if the odds are against me.

Marie Curie couldn't get into the University of Warsaw because of gender restrictions, so she attended Sorbonne University at the age of 24. "In Paris, she felt unprepared but exhilarated."[78] The university had only a handful of women, 23 out of a population of 1,800 students, so the odds of her succeeding were stacked against her.[79]

Marie beat the odds and made history as the first person to win two Nobel Prizes. Her first, she shared with her husband in 1903. Then, she went on to win a second in 1911.[80] At of the time of this writing, she is still the only person to have received Nobel Prizes in two scientific categories. What if Marie had quit because of her gender or after her husband, Pierre, died in 1906?

After his death, Sorbonne invited Marie to take over Pierre's physics class and become the director of the laboratory. She was the first woman ever to teach at the university and this brought other women to the school who were interested in learning science.[81] She left a remarkable legacy.

Though her challenges were immense, she pushed through the adversity, which was a testament to her resilience. Against all odds, she achieved success.

Takeaway: Stick with it.

"Life is not easy for any of us. But what of that?
We must have perseverance and above all confidence
in ourselves. We must believe that we are gifted
for something and that this thing must be attained."
— MARIE CURIE

I am stronger
for facing adversity.

Adversity can be the spark, or the fire, for personal change. It pushes us beyond our comfort zones, so that we will make a change. Because without it, we may remain stagnant.

Whatever the adversity, it's a part of who you are, however, it doesn't have to be your whole story. As Maya Angelou said, "I can be changed by what happens to me. But I refuse to be reduced by it." Don't let adversity diminish you. Let it shape and strengthen you.

Takeaway: Use adversity to your advantage.

"It's your reaction to adversity, not adversity itself that determines how your life's story will develop."

— DIETER F. UCHTDORF

My struggles lead to deep understanding.

Through our struggles, we become more connected to our own humanity. We foster kindness and empathy. These tough times provide a window into the challenges that others face in their lives. How can we truly comprehend something if we haven't endured it? I saw a quote on Trent Shelton's Facebook page that said, "The most beautiful souls are those who survive the fire and come back with water to help those still struggling within it."[82]

Experience is a brilliant teacher and it is through our difficulties that we receive some of our most valuable lessons. The hardships we face carve depth into who we are, shaping compassion and strength that wouldn't exist without the struggle. It's in carrying these lessons forward and helping others that we shift from merely enduring life to actively expanding through it.

This allows us to see life as an unfolding path rather than a fixed destination. Every setback becomes part of an evolving journey—one that reveals new possibilities beyond the pain. When we start taking brave steps, resistance softens, confidence rises, and resilience builds as challenges turn into choices. With self-awareness, we honor and truly get to know ourselves.

Takeaway: Focus, release, and grow a better mindset.

"Nothing is more beautiful than the smile
that has struggled through the tears."
— DEMI LOVATO

Mindset Playlist

- "On Top Of The World" by Imagine Dragons
- "Stronger" by Kelly Clarkson
- "Roar" by Katy Perry
- "Brave" by Sara Bareilles
- "Unwritten" by Natasha Bedingfield
- "Fight Song" by Rachel Platten
- "The Climb" by Miley Cyrus
- "Try Everything" by Shakira
- "Try" by P!nk
- "Get Over It" by Eagles
- "Shake It Off" by Taylor Swift
- "Good Day Sunshine" by The Beatles
- "Best Day Of My Life" by American Authors
- "Lovely Day" by Bill Withers
- "Beautiful Day" by U2
- "What A Wonderful World" by Louis Armstrong
- "Put A Little Love In Your Heart" by Jackie DeShannon
- "This Is Me" from *The Greatest Showman*
- "Ain't No Mountain High Enough" by Marvin Gaye and Tammi Terrell

Happy Playlist

- "Happy" by Pharrell Williams
- "Don't Worry, Be Happy" by Bobby McFerrin
- "Walking on Sunshine" by Katrina & The Waves
- "Living in the Moment" by Jason Mraz
- "Good Vibrations" by The Beach Boys
- "Let's Go Crazy" by Prince
- "CAN'T STOP THE FEELING!" by Justin Timberlake
- "I'm Coming Out" by Diana Ross
- "Girls Just Want to Have Fun" by Cyndi Lauper
- "Take Me To The Pilot" by Sir Elton John
- "September" by Earth, Wind & Fire
- "Good as Hell" by Lizzo
- "Happy People" by Little Big Town

Thank You

I want to express my gratitude to all the readers, listeners, and personal growth enthusiasts who have been with me throughout this journey. I am forever grateful and honored to walk alongside you.

If you enjoyed this book, please take a few moments to leave a review or star rating on Amazon, Goodreads, Barnes & Noble, Bookshop.org, or wherever you hang out. I really appreciate the support! It also helps others in their reading journey.

Notes

CHAPTER 1: HAPPINESS

1. Robby Berman, "Happiness Can Be Learned But It May Take Practicing 7 Habits," *Medical News Today*, March 17, 2024, https://www.medicalnewstoday.com/articles/happiness-can-be-learned-but-it-may-take-practicing-7-habits

2. "Dopamine," *Cleveland Clinic*, Last reviewed on 03/23/2022, accessed August 25, 2025, https://my.clevelandclinic.org/health/articles/22581-dopamine

3. NYU, "New and Diverse Experiences Linked to Enhanced Happiness," news release, May 18, 2020, https://www.nyu.edu/about/news-publications/news/2020/may/new-and-diverse-experiences-linked-to-enhanced-happiness--new-st.html

4. Ibid.

5. Laura Ferreri, et al. "Dopamine Modulates the Reward Experiences Elicited by Music," *PubMed Central*, January 22, 2019, https://pmc.ncbi.nlm.nih.gov/articles/PMC6397525/

6. Maureen Salamon, "Music as Medicine," *Harvard Health Publishing*, September 1, 2024, https://www.health.harvard.edu/mind-and-mood/music-as-medicine

7. "Keep Your Brain Young With Music," *John Hopkins Medicine*, accessed August 25, 2025, https://www. hopkinsmedicine.org/health/wellness-and-prevention/ keep-your-brain-young-with-music

8. Lawrence Robinson, Melinda Smith, M.A. and Jeane Sefal, Ph.D., "Laughter is the Best Medicine," *HelpGuide*, Last updated or reviewed on May 16, 2025, https://www.helpguide.org/mental-health/ wellbeing/laughter-is-the-best-medicine

9. Nicholas Coles, "Posing Smiles Can brighten Our Mood," *Stanford Report*, October 20, 2022, https://news.stanford.edu/stories/2022/10/ posing-smiles-can-brighten-mood

10. Ibid.

11. Gina Vild, "The Benefits of Reliving Your Happy Memories," *Psychology Today*, March 30, 2023, https://www.psychologytoday. com/us/blog/a-buoyant-life/202303/ the-benefits-of-reliving-your-happy-memories

12. Ibid.

13. Arthur C. Brooks and Oprah Winfrey, *Build The Life You Want*, (New York: Portfolio/Penguin Random House LLC, 2023), 9-11.

14. Bryan E. Robinson, Ph.D., "A New Study Links Pessimism to Earlier Death," *Psychology Today*, August 2, 2020, https://www.psychologytoday. com/gb/blog/the-right-mindset/202008/ new-study-links-pessimism-earlier-death

CHAPTER 2: FEAR

15. Merriam-Webster Dictionary, s.v. "Fear," accessed August 25, 2025, https://www.merriam-webster.com/dictionary/fear

16. Dr. Rick Hanson, "Confronting the Negativity Bias," *Dr. Rick Hanson*, October 26, 2010, https://rickhanson.com/how-your-brain-makes-you-easily-intimidated/

17. Nadia Kounang, "What's the Science Behind Fear," *CNN Health*, October 29, 2016, https://www.cnn.com/2015/10/29/health/science-of-fear/

18. WomensMedia, "How Your Subconscious Mind Is Running Your Life And How To Fix It," *Forbes*, August 3, 2020, https://www.forbes.com/sites/womensmedia/2020/08/03/how-your-subconscious-mind-is-running-your-life-and-how-to-fix-it/

19. Jessica Koehler, Ph.D., "Why Most Crave Connection—and Why Some of Us Don't," *Psychology Today*, September 12, 2024, https://www.psychologytoday.com/us/blog/beyond-school-walls/202408/why-we-crave-connection-and-why-some-of-us-dont

20. John Amodeo, "Deconstructing the Fear of Rejection: What Are We Really Afraid Of?" *PsychCentral*, March 17, 2014, https://psychcentral.com/blog/deconstructing-the-fear-of-rejection-what-are-we-really-afraid-of#1

21. Ibid.

22. Merriam-Webster Dictionary, s.v. "Bravery," accessed August 25, 2025. https://www.merriam-webster.com/dictionary/bravery

23. Jaimal Rogis, "Baby Steps: The Best Way to Overcome Your Greatest Fear," *LifeHacker*, January 8, 2013, https://lifehacker.com/baby-steps-the-best-way-to-overcome-your-greatest-fear-5973996

24. Ibid.

25. Sarah Gershman, "To Overcome Your Fear of Public Speaking, Stop Thinking About Yourself," *Harvard Business Review*, September 17, 2019, https://hbr.org/2019/09/to-overcome-your-fear-of-public-speaking-stop-thinking-about-yourself

26. Ibid.

27. Ibid.

28. Ibid.

CHAPTER 3: FOCUS

29. Diana Raab, Ph.D., "Calming the Monkey Mind," *Psychology Today*, February 14, 2025, https://www.psychologytoday.com/us/blog/the-empowerment-diary/201709/calming-the-monkey-mind

30. "Autopilot Britian," *Mark and Spencer*, accessed August 25, 2025, https://corporate.marksandspencer.com/sites/marksandspencer/files/Annual%20reports/2017/autopilot-britain-whitepaper.pdf

31. Ibid.

32. Ibid.

33. Kermit Pattison, "Worker Interrupted: The Cost of Task Switching," *Fast Company*, July 28, 2008, https://www.fastcompany.com/944128/worker-interrupted-cost-task-switching

34. "Multitasking: Switching Costs," *American Psychological Association*, accessed August 25, 2025, https://www.apa.org/topics/research/multitasking

35. Jory MacKay, "Single-Tasking: How to Focus on One Thing at a Time, Get More Done, and Feel Less Stressed," *Rescue Time*, accessed August 25, 2025, https://blog.rescuetime.com/single-tasking/

36. Sofia Moutinho, "Edison was Right: Waking Right After Drifting Off to Sleep Can Boost Creativity," *Science*, December 8, 2021, https://www.science.org/content/article/edison-was-right-waking-right-after-drifting-sleep-can-boost-creativity

37. Ibid.

CHAPTER 4: BELIEFS

38. Jennice Vilhauer, "How Your Thinking Creates Your Reality," *Psychology Today*, September 27, 2020, https://www.psychologytoday.com/us/blog/living-forward/202009/how-your-thinking-creates-your-reality

39. Ibid.

40. Mia Primeau, "Your Powerful, Changeable Mindset," *Stanford Report*, September 15, 2021,

https://news.stanford.edu/stories/2021/09/
mindsets-clearing-lens-life

41. Ibid.

42. Keith M. Bellizzi, "Cognitive Biases and Brain
Biology Help Explain Why Facts Don't Change
Minds," *The Conversation*, August 11, 2022, https://
theconversation.com/cognitive-biases-and-brain-
biology-help-explain-why-facts-dont-change-
minds-186530

43. Ibid.

44. Talk of the Nation, "Bet You Didn't Notice
'The Invisible Gorilla'," presented by Neal
Conan, aired May 19, 2010, on NPR, https://
www.npr.org/2010/05/19/126977945/
bet-you-didnt-notice-the-invisible-gorilla

45. Ibid.

46. Brian Tracy, "Subconcious Mind Power Explained,"
Brain Tracy, accessed August 25, 2025, https://
www.briantracy.com/blog/personal-success/
understanding-your-subconscious-mind/

47. Judith E. Pierson, "The Power of the Subconscious
Mind," *ResearchGate*, November 9, 2022, https://www.
researchgate.net/publication/365211107_The_Power_
of_the_Subconscious_Mind

48. Steven Jay Lynn, James Evans, Jean-Roch Laurence,
Scott O Lilienfeld, "What Do People Believe
About Memory? Implications for the Science and
Pseudoscience of Clinical Practice," *PubMed Central*,

December 2015, https://pmc.ncbi.nlm.nih.gov/articles/PMC4679162/

49. Maria Paul, Your Memory is Like The Telephone Game," *Northwestern Now*, September 19, 2012, https://news.northwestern.edu/stories/2012/09/your-memory-is-like-the-telephone-game/

50. Ibid.

51. Ulrich Boser, "The Power of the Pygmalion Effect," *American Progress*, October 6, 2014, https://www.americanprogress.org/article/the-power-of-the-pygmalion-effect/.

CHAPTER 5: GROWTH MINDSET

52. Jessica A. Kent, "Is It Time To Leave Your Comfort Zone? How Leaving Can Spark Positive Change," *Harvard Summer School*, August 28, 2023, https://summer.harvard.edu/blog/leaving-your-comfort-zone/

53. Ibid.

54. Ibid.

55. Adam Grant, *Hidden Potential*, (New York: Penguin Random House LLC, 2023), 55.

56. Adam Grant, *Hidden Potential*, (New York: Penguin Random House LLC, 2023), 56.

CHAPTER 6: SELF-AWARENESS

57. Dana Talesnik, "Eurich Explores Why Self-Awareness Matters," NIH Record, June 28,

2019, https://nihrecord.nih.gov/2019/06/28/
eurich-explores-why-self-awareness-matters

58. Ibid.

59. Elizabeth Perry, "How to develop self-awareness
and unlock your full potential," *BetterUp*, February
6, 2025, https://www.betterup.com/blog/
what-is-self-awareness

60. Dana Talesnik, "Eurich Explores Why Self-
Awareness Matters," NIH Record, June 28,
2019, https://nihrecord.nih.gov/2019/06/28/
eurich-explores-why-self-awareness-matters

61. James R. Bailey and Scheherazade Rehman,
"Don't Underestimate The Power of Self-
Reflection," *Harvard Business Review*,
March 4, 2022, https://hbr.org/2022/03/
dont-underestimate-the-power-of-self-reflection

CHAPTER 7: VISUALIZATION

62. "Reality or Illusion? The Human Battle with
Distinguishing Imagination from Reality," *Neuroscience
News*, April 21, 2023, https://neurosciencenews.com/
reality-illusion-brain-23075/

63. Ibid.

64. Ibid.

65. Joe Puentes, "Visualization Techniques for Athletes:
Boosting Performance Through Mental Imagery,"
Performance Psychology Center, March 13, 2024,

https://www.performancepsychologycenter.com/post/
visualization-techniques-and-mental-imagery

66. Ibid.

67. OWN, "What Oprah Winfrey Learned from Jim
Carrey," *Oprah's Life Class*, October 13, 2011,
YouTube Video, 3:49, https://www.youtube.com/
watch?v=nPU5bjzLZX0

CHAPTER 8: CONFIDENCE

68. John Sisi, "Common Sense About Batting Slumps,"
American Baseball Coaches Association, May/June 2022,
https://www.abca.org/magazine/magazine/2022-3-
May_June/Inside_Interview_Batting_Slumps.aspx

69. Amy Morin, "How to Be More Confident:
9 Tips That Work," *Verywell Mind*, April
25, 2024, https://www.verywellmind.com/
how-to-boost-your-self-confidence-4163098

70. Carol Kinsey Goman, "The Most Important
Body Language Signal For Success," *Forbes*,
November 7, 2013, https://www.forbes.
com/sites/carolkinseygoman/2013/11/07/
the-most-important-body-language-signal-for-success/

71. Ibid.

72. John Giannini, "Building Confidence Through past
Success," *Human Kinetics*, accessed August 25, 2025,
https://canada.humankinetics.com/blogs/excerpt/
building-confidence-through-past-success

73. Amy Morin, "How to Be More Confident: 9 Tips That Work," *Verywell Mind*, April 25, 2024, https://www.verywellmind.com/how-to-boost-your-self-confidence-4163098

CHAPTER 9: ACCEPTANCE

74. Dana Talesnik, "Eurich Explores Why Self-Awareness Matters," NIH Record, June 28, 2019, https://nihrecord.nih.gov/2019/06/28/eurich-explores-why-self-awareness-matters
75. Ibid.

CHAPTER 10: RESILIENCE

76. "Christopher Reeve," *Christopher and Dana Reeve Foundation*, accessed August 25, 2025, https://www.christopherreeve.org/community/about-us/about-christopher-reeve/
77. Dictionary, American Psychological Association, s.v. "Grit," accessed 25, 2025, https://dictionary.apa.org/grit
78. "Marie Curie," *The Nobel Prize*, accessed August 25, 2025, https://www.nobelprize.org/stories/women-who-changed-science/marie-curie
79. Michele Feder, "Marie Curie: Chemistry, Physics, and Radioactivity," *Kahn Academy*, accessed August 25, 2025.

80. "Marie Curie," *The Nobel Prize*, accessed August 25, 2025, https://www.nobelprize.org/stories/women-who-changed-science/marie-curie

81. Deborah Unger, Natalia Sánchez Loayza, The Lost Women of Science Initiative, "Marie Curie's Mentorship Led to Networks of Support for Female Scientists," *Scientific American*, April 24, 2025, https://www.scientificamerican.com/article/marie-curies-mentorship-led-to-networks-of-support-for-female-scientists/

82. Trent Shelton (@Trent Shelton), "The most beautiful souls are those who survive the fire and come back with water to help those still struggling within it," Facebook, March 4, 2025, https://www.facebook.com/LikeTrentShelton/posts/the-most-beautiful-souls-are-those-who-survive-the-fire-and-come-back-with-water/1186303979527326/

Index

CHAPTER 2: FEAR

CHAPTER 3: FOCUS

CHAPTER 4: BELIEFS

CHAPTER 5: GROWTH MINDSET

CHAPTER 8: CONFIDENCE

CHAPTER 9: ACCEPTANCE

CHAPTER 10: RESILIENCE

About the Author

LYNN LOK-PAYNE is the award-winning author of *Wake Up! Change Up! Rise Up!: Practical Tools for Personal Transformation*, which won the prestigious IBPA Book Award, and *Speak This Not That: Positive Affirmations to Have a Better Day*.

As a former CEO turned mindset expert, Lynn uses evidence-based tools to motivate others to become the next chapter of who they are meant to be by creating more empowering narratives for their lives. When not writing, she can be found curled up with a good book, traveling to new locales, and attending concerts.

CONNECT ONLINE
Social Media: @LynnLokPayne
Books and Website: www.LynnLokPayne.com

More From
Lynn Lok-Payne

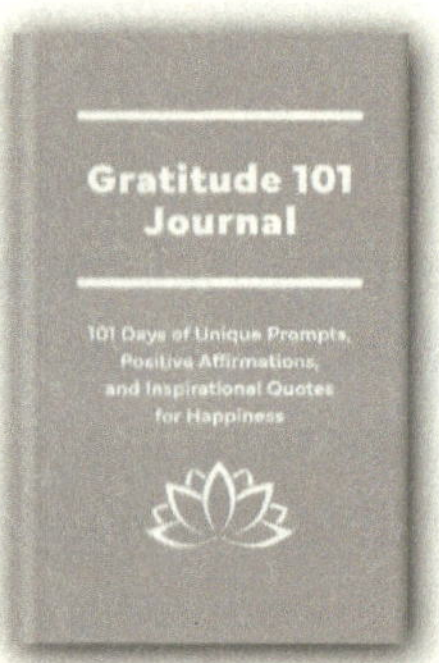

CONNECT ONLINE

Follow @LynnLokPayne

Claim a free gratitude guide and more life tools at: LynnLokPayne.com